Motherless Child

stories from a life

by

Sarah Gordon Weathersby

This story is true, as well as I can remember it.   Names were changed to protect the privacy of the individuals. Some events were combined for the sake of the flow of the story. The movie for the Christmas Show at Radio City Music Hall in 1963 was "Charade," and not "Mondo Cane" which we saw at another time at a theater in New Jersey.

Published by Sarah Weathersby

ISBN 978-0-6152-1294-4

Printed in the United States of America.

Cover design by Cynthia M. Colbert

Dedicated
To Karen Teal
To answer all the hard questions
To Joshua
For not giving up
To Mark
God grant you peace

Acknowledgements

I am the product of all who came before me. I am indebted to God and my family for all lessons, and all blessings. Sometimes the lessons were hard, or I failed until I got it right. God blessed me anyway.

There were many teachers along the way who helped me intentionally, and there were some who left me with a lesson in spite of themselves. I thank God for them all. There were friends who traveled this road with me for a long time when it was hard and when it was easy. God's blessings are with us always. Mother told me in a dream that she would always be with me. It was her dream for me to publish a book. It was a long time coming, and I hope I have made her proud.

Thank you to my friends Mary Cannie and Karen Long, for reading and critiquing along the way. And my dear husband, for reading until you couldn't read again, one more time. For your support, even in the late hours when I had to fix it one more last time, Sweetie, I thank you.

Thank you to my online communities, and writing groups who encouraged and helped me. And to all the dear friends who waited so long for the completion of this book, you will never know how your comments kept me motivated in that midnight hour. Thank you, Cynthia Marie for your work of art. I found a kindred spirit in you, even though we have never met in person. You read me very well.

And to my children, this is my story, and it's your story. I hope I haven't embarrassed you with it.

Stories

Prologue

I never thought I would find Teal's father almost forty years after I last heard from him. Jimmy is such a common name that I didn't even try searching on the internet until the last remaining volume of my journal fell out of a box of tax receipts. I had written in the journal that he had married Paula. That turned out to be just enough information to find him as an associate with a full page on the Howard University website that had his photograph and enough other information for me to find a phone number as well. I was trembling when I left the message, "You will remember me as Sarah Gordon. I have some exciting news to tell you."

He returned the call the next day, but he needed his teen-aged son to help him with the call. He had had a stroke that affected the speech center of his brain. His speech wasn't at all slurred, but it was difficult for him to put the words together especially over the phone. He remembered me, of course, and he seemed happy to hear I had found our daughter. Paula came on the line to explain that he might understand it all better if I wrote him a letter. That was going to make it easier for me as well; I was shaky, trying to say the right things, since I didn't want to lose this contact. Teal wanted to meet her father.

It had been only three months since I had met our daughter, the child I gave up for adoption so long ago. I had tried many years to find her, and even signed up with the Adoption Registry, but until she decided to look for her birth mother, they would not give out the contact information. The idea of looking for her birth parents never crossed her mind until she became a mother herself. And now she wanted to know why I gave her up.

I called Teal to tell her that I had found her father. She seemed relieved that another piece of the puzzle was completed, and happy to know there was more family for her to meet. She had already developed a strong connection with my son Joshua through regular phone calls, and she hoped to have that same connection with Jimmy's daughters. I wrote to Jimmy, and sent photos to Paula and their daughters by email. The following month she met all of her long-lost family on both sides, giving her the brothers and sisters and uncles and aunts as she had never had and always wished for.

The experience of finding Teal has been such a blessing, but also caused me to replay that time through my memory. I hardly remember the girl I was back then, and it's difficult to sort out all the thought processes and reasons I gave myself. When I looked back over my life, I often wondered if I should regret giving a child away. How could I regret, when I didn't know how the story ended? I knew that at the time, I could not have provided for Teal what two loving parents could give her. Now that I know they gave her more than I ever could have, I know it was the right decision for that time, and I have no regrets.

Look it up in the Dictionary

Morning awoke to the sound of Daddy's coughing. He smoked a pipe with Prince Albert tobacco. Sometimes he would roll a cigarette from the same stuff, so he was always hacking in the morning. Even with all the other din in the house, with four brothers going out and coming in from their morning paper routes, and vying for their turn in the bathroom, the first sound I heard was Daddy's coughing. Daddy would get the house moving, starting the fire in the stove downstairs, and getting bacon and grits cooking. I slept in the same bed with my sister Toni. She complained that my teeth grinding kept her awake at night. And if I wet the bed, she would make me get the clean sheets to change it in the middle of the night, stuffing newspapers over the wet spot in the mattress so we could get back to sleep.

With one bathroom for nine people, it meant precision timing to keep the schedule. By doubling up, one person could wash in the sink, while another took a bath. In the winter there was never enough hot water, so Daddy would have kettles boiling, placing them in the bathroom, ready for us. Mother had to be on her way to the school where she taught English and typing before my brothers went off to school. Since Daddy was a priest, he could stay home with me and Toni during the day.

By the time I was two years old, Mother would dress me and Toni in the same clothes. Maybe Mother thought it was cute, or maybe it was just convenient to buy two of the same thing, one sized 2, and one sized 6X, when she ordered from the Montgomery Ward catalog. It was always a surprise when the box arrived, with two of each outfit. Toni would whine that she didn't want to dress like a baby, while I crooned with glee, "We could be TRINS," as I said, meaning "twins."

My most vivid early memory was Christmas a few months after I turned two years old. It was 1947, and I was the baby of the family. My sister Toni was six years old, and we had four doting brothers. Michael was eleven, George thirteen, Ronald fourteen, and Bobby at sixteen was a senior in high school. (Yes, my Mother survived having four sons born within five years.) At that time there were only eleven years of public school for Negroes in Petersburg, Virginia. Bobby would start college the next year at Virginia State College, where all of my brothers and Toni would eventually attend. My oldest sister LaVerne had graduated from St. Augustine's College in Raleigh, NC the year I was born, and by the Christmas of 1947 she had married and had a daughter of her own, my niece Lynne.

My brothers enjoyed participating in the fantasy for me,

and that year they came home on Christmas Eve wanting me out of the way so they could wrap gifts, told me I had to go to bed because they heard sleigh bells in the sky, and sent me off to bed clutching my favorite rag-doll, Sally. The next morning, there were animal footprints through the house, that my brothers said were made by the reindeer. I found out years later they had dragged the dog through the dirt, and walked him through the house.

The big gift for me was a new Sally. I had dragged the old one everywhere so that she had her stuffing falling out in places, and the clothes she once had were gone. My brothers had tried to make me give up my Sally, so the new one was to be a replacement. She was exactly the same doll, just new. I carried the new Sally around for a while, and she made old Sally look so pitiful that I gave her up. Since the new Sally could never take her place, I found an imaginary playmate, to take the place of the real Sally.

My brothers all had some kind of job growing up. Each of them started out carrying newspapers and as the next one came along the older one would pass the newspaper route to the younger brother, and the older one would get some better odd job. All their money was given to Mother who kept a journal of how much money each one had in the fund. They could take money out for clothes and things they needed for school. Anything else they wanted they had to vote on. When Michael found an old piano that he wanted to buy for fifteen dollars they had to vote on it. Now sixty-some years later there is some disagreement about whether the brothers did in fact agree to the purchase, or Mother decided that a piano was a good idea. It was an old upright that had been painted some blue/green color, and most of the keys stuck. All the same, my brother used that old piano to learn to play. It was so ugly Mother made him put it out on the back porch, and in winter he had to play with his gloves on. Eventually we did have a "real" piano that sat in the living room.

My brothers used their newspaper money to buy the assortment of things we had for entertainment. They had a movie projector with a collection of cartoons reels. There was one in which Emmett Kelly's clown face would appear piece by piece, the mouth, the eyes, the ears. Before it got to the hat, I would run screaming from the room. It didn't take much to scare me; I was even afraid of my brothers' socks. Argyle socks were in fashion, and Ronald especially liked to hike up his pants leg to show me his socks. He knew that I thought the diamond designs were part of his leg. I remember thinking his legs had been transformed into snakeskin, and I could see the snakes crawling up his leg.

I don't remember much about the first house I lived in, except that it had a front and back porch, and when it rained, the yard flooded. My brothers would create a kind of current in the water that flowed around the house, and they would float toy boats from the front porch, and run through the house to the back to pick them up, only to take them back to the front to float again.

In the spring we had chickens. We lived in the city of Petersburg, but we had chickens. The boys would buy baby chicks in the spring and build a chicken coop. They were such dumb birds that didn't know how to go in out of the rain, and somebody would have to go out and run them into the coop. When the hens started laying, they would lay eggs anywhere and everywhere. If we found eggs we never knew how old they were or if they were fresh.

Things got particularly exciting when Michael brought a duck home in his newspaper bag. He said the duck followed him home. So they built a separate coop for the duck, and named him Mandrake. Mandrake was a mean old duck. If a bird came to his water bucket for a sip of water, it was the end of the bird because Mandrake swallowed it whole. You could see the outline of the bird going down his gullet. My brother would let the duck out of the coop, but kept him from getting away by tying a cord on his ankle. The bird would fly anyway, with my brother holding the end of the string like a kite.

My brother Bobby was the author of all nicknames. He

was Robert, Jr., so his nickname was already a given. George became "Woody" because he liked to jump up and down and make the noise like Woody Woodpecker in the cartoons. Michael's nickname was the most creative, "Richard." Daddy was a fair-skinned man with straight hair. Mother was much darker, and as a result of their union, the seven of us children were a range of colors in between. Michael had the misfortune of being the youngest of the four brothers, and was subject to being picked on and teased anyway, but when the brothers decided that he was darker than anybody else in the family, they would tell him he was adopted. They didn't dare call him "black" because Mother wouldn't stand for it, so they named him for Richard Wright, the author of "Black Boy." And I, since I was born shortly after the capture of the Japanese Generalissimo, Tojo, I was so named. Bobby took the first look at me, and said, "She looks just like Tojo." And so it stuck. Even family friends and church members knew me as "Tojo."

Daddy was the rector of St. Stephen's Episcopal Church in Petersburg when I was born. Daddy and Mother were both over forty years old by then. After rearing six children before me, they didn't require as much of me as they had my older siblings.

"Parents just get tired," Mother would say.

All that they didn't require of me directly, I learned to demand of myself by being a Gordon.

MOTHERLESS CHILD

We lived in the rectory next to the church, and I was born there. The rectory was bound on one side by the church, the Gem Movie Theater on the other, and the Wiss scissors factory on the back. Across the street was a store that sold groceries, and next to it was a place that sold beer. This was the Negro business district, and it was a busy street. By the time I was four or five, I would ride my tricycle up and down Halifax Street in front of the church. At first Daddy would watch me, then he gave me instructions that I could only go to the left as far as the corner to Owens' Cleaners. I wasn't supposed to go to the right past the Gem Theater, because depending on the time of day there might be crowds of people waiting for the movie, or going in to buy a hot dog for ten cents at the snack bar inside. Eventually Daddy left me to ride on my own. I would ride, pedaling as hard and fast as I could, and I didn't notice I had passed the corner and was heading down another street. At first I panicked, but I kept riding. Since it was a short city block, I soon discovered I was back on Halifax Street where I started.

After that first time I became more adventurous, and would ride around the block whenever nobody was watching. I didn't have to cross a street, so I felt safe, but still very grown up. I remember the exhilaration I felt at making the wheels turn faster than I could walk. Even then I was independent and a loner, who didn't want to have someone watching me all the time. One day when I was riding, I passed a house with a picket fence, and there was a little girl sitting on the porch. I stopped riding and spoke to her, and we talked a little bit about riding my tricycle. Then it became a regular part of my ride around the block, and I would stop and talk to the little girl on the porch.

One day while we were talking, the little girl's mother came out and scolded me for talking to the little girl. "You don't belong on this street." I rode away frightened and crying. When I got home, I didn't want to tell Daddy I had been off Halifax Street, but he could see that I was crying and I told him about that mean old lady that scared me away. He asked if she was white. I hadn't noticed before, but she was. Daddy explained, "They don't want us on that street, so you should stay on Halifax Street like you were told."

After that awakening, I started to notice who was white, and who was not in my fairly protected world. Now I would listen to the conversations in the house more alertly, and hear about my brothers' close calls when they found themselves in the wrong part of town at night. When Toni started school, she was often chased home down that same street with the little girl on the porch. She could have taken a different route, but it was like Toni to stand up to those white kids chasing her. Daddy made sure Toni and I had places to go where we never saw a "White only" sign, even to the other side of town to Pocahontas Park where we could play on the swings and the slide, and drink from the water fountain without a sign of color.

I was not aware of any racial tension in my protected world until the day Mother couldn't vote. She had left work early to get back before the polls closed. The polling place for our neighborhood was the corner store where Mother had to wait in line almost an hour before they told her she couldn't vote because she didn't have her receipt for paying the poll tax. Mother came home almost in tears, not from hurt, but from anger. When she came in slamming doors, all of us came running because we never saw Mother like that before.

Then Ronald who was always in trouble with saying the wrong thing about religion or politics said, "But Mother, you were going to vote for Eisenhower!" Ronald was a member of the Americans for Democratic Action at Virginia State, and didn't understand how our parents could be Republican.

Then he proceeded to expound on the virtues of Adlai Stevenson. "He's a new breed of Democrat, not at all like the Dixie-crats we have in Congress." Mother listened. Then Ronald asked Daddy if he had voted. Daddy left the room without saying anything, since he had been successful in voting for Eisenhower.

I was very attentive to family discussions, even when I couldn't get a word in edgewise. I didn't always understand what they were talking about, but once I got the chance I would ask. Such was the case when there had been an assault in the neighborhood, and all the family was talking about the girl who had been raped. My brothers were sure that a white man had done it, and feared the police would never even bother to charge anybody with a crime. When I finally got my turn to ask, I asked, "What is raked," since that was what I understood them to say. Then Mother tried to explain without getting into very much detail, that it was a terrible thing a bad man might do to a girl. Since she didn't correct my saying, "raked," I still had in my mind a picture of a garden rake, and a poor girl being beat up and scratched with the metal prongs. It was frightening enough that I didn't ask for any more details.

By the time I was eight, Daddy was given a new assignment. Instead of being rector of St. Stephen's he was assigned to three churches on a circuit. One church met first and third Sundays, one met second and fourth Sundays, and one little church only had service when there was a fifth Sunday. On Easter he would go to all of the churches, and he wouldn't get home until dark.

Instead of being assigned to a rectory to live in, we were given the house that once served as the President's House for Bishop Payne Divinity School there in Petersburg. Daddy had graduated from Bishop Payne some years before I was born.

Around 1950, the Episcopal Church decided not to continue having a segregated seminary, merged that faculty and student body into Virginia Theological Seminary, and then pretty much abandoned the facility there on West Street. The school consisted of a large building that had dormitory space, classrooms, library and dining room, all under one roof. There was a small chapel on the corner next to the house where we lived.

It seemed like such a large house at the time, but it was packed tight with the eight of us. There were only three bedrooms and one bath. Mother and Daddy had their room, and Toni and I had another. At first all the boys shared the third room using two sets of bunk beds. By the time my sister LaVerne returned home with her daughter Lynne, Bobby and Ronald had joined the Army. Then the room assignment was in constant flux. Lynne shared the room with Toni and me, until Toni decided she was grown enough to share a room with LaVerne. There was a sofa bed in the dining room for George, and the back porch had been enclosed so Michael stayed out there with his piano, even though it wasn't heated. We thought it was fun to have two staircases. If somebody came to the front door that we didn't want to see, we could sneak down the back stairs to the kitchen and out the back door. When Toni wasn't ready for a boyfriend who came, she could go down to the kitchen and iron her dress, go back upstairs, and appear all fresh and pressed in the front hall.

We called it "the Hall" because it was separate from the living room and dining room. The idea of a family room didn't exist back then, at least not for us. The front stairs came down into the Hall, with a landing that flourished down to two wide steps. Mother liked to have her picture taken on that landing, and pretend she was an elegant lady of the manor. When we finally got TV, it was set up in the Hall, and the downstairs telephone was at a desk in the Hall. When we watched TV, especially on hot summer nights, when my niece Lynne would be with us for the whole summer, Lynne and I would stretch out on those bottom two steps, on the bare wood because it was cool to lie there. We had a big kitchen where we could play jacks on the floor with our legs splayed out to mark the game space in front of the refrigerator.

When we moved into that house, Daddy had the keys to the main building across the street as well. Daddy said we could get furniture for our house, which had only the little furniture we had brought with us when we moved from the rectory at St. Stephens.

We were like marauders, getting bunk beds, tables, chairs, and books. And the library was the big find. Such books as we had never owned, encyclopedias, and unabridged dictionaries with oak book stands. It didn't matter that they were much out of date, published in 1934. We had recently learned to play Scrabble, and with those huge dictionaries, it ratcheted our play up to a new level. We used those blue metal dormitory sets in our bedrooms, and some of those pieces are still in the family in somebody's house even today.

Now when Mother or my brothers would tell me to look it up in the dictionary, I didn't mind anymore that they were avoiding having to explain something to me, because I knew I could start my search for words and each new definition would lead me on a search for more words. Sometimes, I would forget what word I started with, and I would spend hours in that dictionary looking for words. If I overheard them talking about "intercourse," and I asked what that was, I could look it up in my 1934 Unabridged Dictionary. Usually I would find another undecipherable word, like "coitus" and it was on!!

It was Toni's Fault

It was Toni's fault that Mrs. Vernon turned out to be so mean to me, but maybe I should thank Mrs. Vernon for sending me to the library as punishment. The last thing Toni would have wanted was for me to learn to read. She didn't even want me to dress like her.

Toni certainly didn't like having me tagging along behind her. But when Toni started to school that February, since her birthday was too late to start in September, there was no way I could go with her. Even when I got up early while it was still dark, took my position in the big old overstuffed brown chair by the stairs, and watched everyone get ready to go to school, they wouldn't let me go along. Most weekday mornings, that was the only place I could see Mother before she went off to teach English at the High School of Disputanta Training School, in Dinwiddie County. My chair was soft and saggy, and just right for a two-year-old to curl up. Sometimes I would fall asleep again while waiting to see everyone off for the day.

Daddy usually dressed in clerics even around the house. After he tried to find something I would eat for breakfast, it was my job to dry the flatware and put it away in the proper spaces in the kitchen drawer.

Now Toni was going off to school, leaving me behind. That first day, I waited most of the morning in my chair for her return. Since first-graders went only half days, she returned soon after I had eaten my lunch. We were so happy to see each other. Toni brought me chocolate drops and showed me her books from school. How could she leave me behind? She was going to learn to read and I wouldn't.

I knew what I had to do, though. I knew where everything was kept in that rectory on Halifax Street. I knew exactly where in the attic to find the old school books. Now that Toni had shown me her books about Dick and Jane, I knew exactly where to find more. Now that I knew they were for learning to read, I could be just like my sister and learn to read, too.

I must have dug around in that old dusty attic for a long time before Daddy started calling, looking for me. "Here I am." And he found me, deep into a pile of reading books, spelling books, and my brothers' algebra and biology books.

"You have to teach me to read," I demanded.

Daddy knew I was lonesome, being without a playmate for the first time in my life. There was no neighborhood with children to play with. Daddy helped me select a book, and promised that after his chores were finished, we would read. It was already our daily routine to read the "Funny Paper." It was only a matter of weeks before I had read every primary reader in the house, and had reversed roles with Daddy, reading the Funny Paper to him.

Maybe it was because I could read, or maybe it was because Daddy was given a committee assignment with the Diocese, but for some reason Mother decided when I was four years old, to take me with her out to the county every day. Toni was in school all day, and would go to the Gem Theater after school to wait for Daddy when he finished his work. Mrs. Ruth Royal, who was a member of our church, was the lady in the box office. Daddy would pay the 10 cents per day admission for Toni for the whole week, and Mrs. Royal would make sure Toni came directly from school and was safe until Daddy arrived. Toni watched the same movies over and over again, until she knew all the dialog from memory. And she saw the episodes of the serials before everybody else who would have to wait until Saturday when Lash LaRue would be rescued from the cliff hanger.

At first I would sit in the back of Mother's English and typing classes, help out with errands, and mostly be bored. That was until Mother's friend Mrs. Johnson, said I could come to her second-grade class. At least I would be around children. I sat in the front of the room, and helped pass out papers and supplies. I could color and cut out things with the class, until I learned the proper way to raise my hand to take a turn at reading. To the little girls in the class, I was a plaything. The little boys made faces because I could read better than some of them. I even participated in the spelling bee one time. I knew how to spell the easy words like cat and dog, but when the teacher called on me to spell "said," I tried to spell it "s-e-d," and had to sit down.

This continued for many weeks until the day Mrs. Johnson stayed in a meeting for two hours at the end of the day, leaving her class unattended except for one girl assigned to "take names." The class had acted up and made enough noise to disturb the teacher across the hall. When Mrs. Johnson came back, she was furious. Since all of the students except me, rode the bus, she couldn't keep them after school, and she promised to punish the whole class the next day. Even at four years old, I knew that punishment meant she would take her special strap from her locked desk drawer and whip the students on their hands. I went to Mother crying that I couldn't be whipped, and I would never go back to school.

I cried so much every morning, that Mother didn't take me back to Disputanta again, and I started school officially the year I turned six.

* * *

Life returned to my usual routine at home with Daddy every day. I was the favorite plaything for my four big brothers, and the object of their hobbies. I helped George organize his plants and leaf collection, and he enjoyed teaching me the names of all the trees in the yard. I was Ronald's photographic model, if I couldn't hide well enough for him to find me. Michael taught me songs, and before I was five years old, I could sing "O Holy Night" in front of the whole church. Bobby brought me some of his Arts and Crafts from school. My favorite was a Hitler puppet he had made.

Mother wanted so much for her youngest, that she did everything to try to bring out whatever talent I might have. Even at four, I had long slender fingers that Mother said were "piano hands." Michael was already taking piano lessons with Mrs. King once a week at her house. Toni had reached the second level of instruction, so Mother thought I was ready to begin the John Thompson beginner book, "Teaching Little Fingers to Play." Daddy took Toni for her lesson, and when it was time to pick her up, he took me along. Mrs. King started me off with only a few minutes, so Daddy could wait until I was finished. She showed me the scales and told me to practice the drill every day so I could go on to the next lesson.

I took pleasure in sitting there on the bench with Mrs. King. She placed my hands just so, and I delighted in being able to follow the drill as she instructed. I went home and practiced. After weeks of lessons, I was finally able to play a simple melody with only my right hand. When we reached the lessons using two hands, it was more difficult for me to follow, and I hated to practice. If I waited too many days after my lesson, I would forget how to place my hands, and I just couldn't get it. When I couldn't hit the right notes, I would cry, and try again, and cry again. It became a painful regimen for me, and for anybody in the house who was listening to my banging and crying. Mother finally couldn't take it anymore and told me I wouldn't be taking any more piano lessons. I was relieved, but years later I wished I had had the maturity to learn to play the piano at four years old.

When I finally started school in Petersburg, I was in the afternoon class for first grade at Giles B. Cook Elementary. Daddy walked me to school everyday until he decided I could handle it alone. Instead of telling me I was old enough to go by myself, one morning he was especially slow getting ready. I waited with my book bag in hand, and nagged him that I would be late for school. It was important to be there in time for lunch, when I could eat my bologna sandwich and have a carton of school chocolate milk. After I had nagged for a while, Daddy told me to go on, and he would catch up. I went off down the street, watching for Daddy to catch up. By the time I reached the corner where I would turn, I could see Daddy leaving the house. He followed me at a distance from there on, and at every turn, I would look back to make sure he was still following me.

There were no major streets to cross and hardly ever a car passing at that time of day anyway. By the time I reached the school, Daddy was not even in sight, so I waited until I could see him, and waved good-bye as I went into the school building. I was on my own from then on. Toni and the other kids in the neighborhood were there after school to walk with me.

My first grade teacher was Mrs. Phillips, who was a member of our church, and Godmother to my friend Yvonne. She was the kind of first grade teacher every parent would want for a child. She was gentle and kind, and all the children loved her. She became fascinated with the fact that I could already read all of the "Dick and Jane" series for first grade, and then she started testing me on more advanced reading books. When I could read those as well, she sent for books from the library at Peabody High School, across the street. I could read everything she gave me.

By second grade, I had earned the reputation for being the teacher's pet. The first day of second grade, Joseph who was with me in Mrs. Phillips class, said loudly, "Sarah's going to be the teacher's pet again!" That was the first time I knew what a teacher's pet was. I knew that Joseph liked to talk too much.

Mrs. Vernon made it clear that there were no pets in her class. She seemed pleased with herself whenever she could mark something wrong on my papers, and she would get angry whenever I asked why my answer was wrong, when the person next to me had the same answer marked as correct. The little boys in the class would howl when that happened. I wasn't trying to contradict her as she said, but I could not stand to get less than 100, especially when my paper was right.

That was the year I became the class cry-baby. It upset me to get less than 100, and I didn't understand how a teacher could not like me. Mrs. Vernon would say I was just trying to get attention. I would try to stop crying, but the more she looked at me with that evil scowl, the more it hurt. Many of the teachers at Giles B. Cook Elementary School knew me from the neighborhood, or from church, and smiled when they saw me, or sometimes said hello to me, but not Mrs. Vernon. Of course, she was equally evil to everyone in the class, but I felt she had singled me out. On the playground, the boys had the rhymes they would make about the "mean old witch."

In the spring, all of Giles B. Cook came together for the May Day program. The planning started months before. That year each of the five grades was assigned a country to represent for May Day. The second grade would represent Japan. The 3 second grade teachers brought all of the classes together in the library one day and told the children that fifteen girls would be selected to dress up like Japanese women for the May Day program. The boys were happy they would not have to be in the program, and they put their heads together in the back of the room to try to guess which girls would be selected. Each of the teachers would select five girls. My friends Alice, Zelma, and Yvonne were selected, and as each name was called, the boys looked at me, and whispered, "You're next." By the time twelve girls had been selected, and Mrs. Vernon had not called my name, one of the other teachers called my name, and I sighed with relief and stood up to join the group.

Then the worst thing happened that I could imagine in my seven-year-old world. Mrs. Vernon whispered something to the other teacher and told me to sit down. Of course I cried, sobbing uncontrollably, until she had to send me to the principal's office. As I left the room, the other girls, even the ones who had not been chosen, patted my back. And I overheard the librarian who was Mrs. Vernon's sister, say to her, "You know you're wrong."

I must have cried the rest of the day, until my eyes and nose were red and swollen. On the way home, all of the children gathered around me, saying how evil that old witch was. When I went home and told everybody, nobody seemed to understand how crushing it was for me. Mother said, "You can't be in everything," and reminded me I had been in the school Easter program in First Grade, and always sang in church. And of course in those days, the teacher's decision was final.

That event changed my life in another way, though. When

it was time for the May Day practice, every afternoon, during class time, all of the second grade classes went to the auditorium to sit while the chosen girls went through their routine. Since it was still so upsetting for me to remember how much it had hurt, I would start crying all over again, and Mrs. Vernon sent me to the library. Mrs. Howard was a sympathetic woman, who put me to work in the library. She showed me how to check books out, how to organize the cards, and put books back on the shelves when they were returned. Then she let me take out as many books as I wanted, when her usual rule was one book a week.

I read voraciously. At first Mrs. Howard steered me to the second grade books, but after I read a dozen or so, I found they were all too easy for me. When she let me check out any book in the library, I read everything I could get my hands on. I read every Bobbsey Twins book in the library, then I continued on fairy tales, and I would read of princes and dragons, and wizards and magic. I so looked forward to my afternoons in the library, that I started getting to school early in the morning to work in the library. By then Mrs. Howard made me her assistant librarian, and sent a note to her sister, Mrs. Vernon to have me come to the library to help whenever I had some "free time." So we got a break from each other, and she stopped being so hard on me.

It was Toni's Fault

Fifty years later, I was sitting in the arena at the CIAA basketball tournament beside my friend Yvonne, and she pointed out the daughters of Mrs. Vernon as they went down the aisle to their seats. The oldest was tall, slim, and aloof like her mother, and that old hurt welled up in my stomach, when Yvonne asked if I remembered Mrs. Vernon. I said, "Yes, and her sister was the Librarian." Yvonne said Mrs. Howard had died, and Mrs. Vernon had Alzheimer's and was in a nursing home. "She caused me major trauma in second grade, and I wrote a whole chapter about her." Yvonne didn't seem surprised at all.

*　*　*

Summertime, and the living was easy. Mother made sure we had enough work to keep us from getting lazy. She had a vegetable garden that we had to tend early in the morning before the sun was too high. Planting and weeding and watering were our daily chores. And her flowers were some rare assortment that she would trade with friends wherever we went to visit. If she saw a plant she thought was pretty, she would ask for a piece and it would be added to the garden. Once she discovered my brother George's green thumb, she would give the little sprig to him to plant. There was some magic in his hands, so he could simply poke a small hole in the dirt, add some water, and push the sprig in. In a few days it would take root, and before long be bushier than the parent plant it had come from. It seemed

George could plant anything. There was even one year when he planted our Christmas tree after Christmas. It was merely a tree the brothers had chopped down while poaching in somebody's woods and brought home on Christmas Eve. It had no root ball, just a clean diagonal cut. George stuck it in the ground and it took root.

After our outside chores, we were free to go to the park or to visit friends. There were few places we could go for planned activities. When my brother Bobby returned from the Korean War, he was stationed at Fort Lee, near Petersburg. He could take us to Lake Jordan which was owned by the military, and was open to all military personnel and their families regardless of race. It seemed, however, there were mostly Negroes on the days we went. One summer they opened it up for the Girl Scouts to have Day Camp. The white troops went for several weeks, and then we had our one week. We had swimming lessons in the lake, and arts and crafts in the picnic area in the shade. Toni and I could earn many of our Girl Scout badges during one week.

Mother liked to go riding in the car, late in the afternoon after dinner. Sometimes we went to Pocahontas Park on the other side of town where there was a slide. Daddy would bring some waxed paper to help make the slide slick enough for us to slide down, otherwise we would get stuck half-way down. Sometimes we would go riding out into the country looking for wild berries. We stayed on the lookout for blackberry bushes growing near the road, and if we found a good one, we would pick enough berries so Mother could make blackberry cobbler. We would go home full of chiggers that would burrow into the pubic joint or into our ankles under our socks. They said if you painted the bumps with nail polish it would suffocate the bug and stop the itching. I never saw a bug come out of the bumps, and they would itch for days.

If we came upon roadside stands selling fruit, Mother would very carefully negotiate the price, considering the freshness and the quality of the fruit. We would laugh to ourselves while we waited for her to acquire some treasure, peaches so big and juicy, we could wash our faces in them. If we ate them without washing the fuzz off, we would itch from the afternoon on until we could go home and scrub. With no air-conditioning and only one fan for the house, we would cool off by taking a bath, powder ourselves dry with talcum, and sit on the porch, or play yard games like Simon Says, Statue, Red light, or we would catch lightning bugs in a jar. When the street lights came on, we knew it was time to go in.

The neighborhood children sometimes had a baseball game in the field across the street. Boys and girls would play together, and everyone would line up to get picked for a team. I didn't know anything at all about baseball, but since Toni would go out to play, I had to be there too. I was always the last to get picked, and they would send me into the outfield. Since I didn't know what was going on, I would just stand and wait, hoping maybe sometime I would get a chance at bat. We didn't have baseball gloves, and there was one precious ball. When my team finally came to bat, I waited and waited, but didn't get a chance at bat unless half the team had to go home for dinner. And then I missed. The only time I got to first base was when I fouled out. I was glad when the street lights came on.

Some evenings we sang together. My favorite was the orchestra song. Since it took me a few years to get the hang of singing a different part from everybody else, I would chime in with the sound of each instrument that I knew. The fiddles they play it, the trumpets they trump ta-da-da trump. The horns they shout it out. The bassoon it makes a point of counterpoint. The drum has no trouble just double-dub-double. Mostly I sang some of everybody's part, and we would all laugh when it seemed to sound the best with all the voices, and we would try to keep it going until George started getting flat like he always did. By that time we had a real piano in the living room, not just the raggedy upright that Michael bought with funds appropriated from the boys' newspaper earnings.

Whenever anybody teased George about his singing, he

would remind us that he won the talent contest at school by singing "Night and Day." Then the real story would be told. Mother was always planning events at the churches where Daddy served, and she would encourage the boys to participate. Everyone had an "act." It was one thing to perform at home, but George decided to take his act to school for the Talent Show. When he hit the first three notes of "Night and Day" the kids in the audience thought it was funny that he was so serious singing off-key and they started to laugh. By the time they settled down, he had reached the next "Night and Day" in the song, equally off-pitch. That set the children to laughing again. As he continued to sing, it was funnier and funnier, so by the time he reached the final "Night and Day" they decided it was a great comedy act, and applauded so loudly, that George won the contest.

*   *   *

Being a Gordon and loving travel was a given. We said it was in the genes passed down from Mother's side of the family. Of course in the days of Jim Crow, travel was limited for a southern black family. Vacation meant visiting relatives, and if members of the family moved away in any direction, the rest would follow making that a new vacation destination. Daddy came along reluctantly most times, but he added his classmates from Morris Brown College and Bishop Payne Divinity School to the resources we had for vacation spots.

We would pack up the whole crew in one car. At that time, LaVerne's daughter, my niece Lynne, was spending summers with us in Petersburg, and Bobby and Ronald had left for the Korean War. So there were seven of us in that old Buick. The back seat was big enough that the smallest child could lie across the back in the window, and watch the stars at night, or sit on the potty on the floor in the back when there was no place where we were allowed to stop for a rest room. We would carry food for breakfast and lunch since there were few places that we could stop to eat, besides being beyond our family budget for all of us to eat somewhere.

I remember the year we went to Canada. We stopped in Philadelphia to visit a friend of Daddy's from seminary. I don't know if they expected so many of us to spend the night, but they were very gracious hosts. It must have been the first time I ever had iced tea. It was a hot summer day and we had been driving a long time without a break. When we arrived, the lady of the house asked if we would like something to drink, and showed us to the kitchen. It was the most beautiful kitchen I had ever seen in person. It was like something out of the movies with a booth in the corner with a red table and red leather seats. The iced tea was exactly the thing to perk us up. She made crab cakes for us to eat, and they were delicious as well.

It was a huge house, and our hosts made places for us all to sleep and we didn't mind at all doubling up or sleeping wherever there was space. They even had telephones in different colors, unlike the all black ones we had at home. It seemed like a fairy tale for that short visit before we went on to New York and Quebec.

When we crossed the border into Canada, the agent asked us where we lived, and where we all were born. Mother and Daddy had been born in Georgia, and had children in born Virginia and Florida and West Virginia where Daddy had served as rector. That was the first time I had heard all the places where we were born, and even at my age I thought we must have seemed like an odd family to have lived so many different places. But they let us into Canada, anyway. We drove through Quebec, paying attention to the signs in French, that George would try to translate based on the French he had in high school. We stopped at a store to buy milk to go with the sandwiches our host in Philadelphia had made for us. We saved that liter bottle to take home as a souvenir. And it seemed the Canadian milk tasted sweeter than the milk back home.

Mother had a dream of going somewhere abroad, and she would say that one day she would go to Cuba. That was before the rise of Fidel Castro, so it might have been possible for someone with the means to travel there. Mother would be proud to know that I lived in Germany for almost a year.

How does a child know?

Spin me around 'til I fell asleep,
Then up the stairs he would carry me,
And I knew for sure, I was loved.
"Dance with my Father"- sung by Luther Vandross

How does a child know when she is loved? Nobody ever said, I love you in our house, and I didn't have a sense of what love was, but I knew everything was right, and it all fit together in our house. I thought I knew that life would always be the same at home with brothers coming and going. As long as Ronald was in town there would be political arguments. As long as Michael was there, there would be singing. Daddy would complain when Michael broke out in singing an aria so loud it would cause our dog Smokey to howl, but I guessed he enjoyed the noise. I know I did, and I thought it would last forever.

There came a time I couldn't seem to please Mother, especially when it came to standing up for myself. Even when Lynne came for the summer. Lynne was my first real playmate – my niece who was born before I was two years old. It seemed that Lynne had more clothes, more toys, more things that she wouldn't share, and we would fight. She even had her own personal bottle of Jergen's lotion that she hoarded so she could apply lotion to her legs anytime she wanted, while I had only Mother's jar of Vaseline. We would fight. I would scratch and Lynne would bite. My brothers thought it was funny enough to take pictures that we can laugh about now. It didn't seem so at the time, especially after Lynne had bit a plug out of my belly, and I ran to Mother to be bandaged. She chastised me for letting someone younger beat me up.

When Lynne and I weren't fighting, we were plotting against Toni. She was always bossing us around, but we had our secret code words that we could say and laugh about her so she would leave us alone. By the time Toni was a teenager, it seemed she was always in trouble with Mother. By then, LaVerne and Lynne had come to live with us full time. She had told Lynne that she had come home to be with Mother who was sick. She didn't tell Lynne or me that she and Lynne's father were getting a divorce. And nobody told me Mother had cancer. I found out about the divorce accidentally when LaVerne left some papers from her lawyer in the kitchen, but I never told Lynne. Lynne knew about the cancer, but she never told me. We didn't fight anymore after that. Each of us had the need to comfort the other, not knowing we both needed comforting. We still had our bond against Toni, not a serious plot, but a cause for giggling way into the night, especially in the summer.

I wasn't so lonely with Lynne around, but I still missed having my mother in my life. There were times when I secretly wished LaVerne was my mother; after all, she was nineteen years older than I was. Suppose she had really given birth to me, and had given me to Mother to raise? I gave up that pipe dream when it came time for getting motherly advice and guidance; it was LaVerne with Lynne, excluding me.

Lynne and I never knew what Toni did that day in summer, but we suspected she said something sassy, that Mother had it out with her. The last time I remember being spanked was when I was a preschooler and probably broke something I shouldn't have touched. I remember Mother picked up the first thing she could get her hands on, and whipped me with a worn out slipper. I cried long and hard as if my heart would break, and I think it broke Mother's heart to hear me. But that day with Toni, she used a shoe and a belt. When Toni wanted to go to her room afterwards, Mother insisted that she straighten up and stay with the rest of the family, watching TV in the front hall. Toni had nothing to say to me and Lynne for weeks after that. It must have been during the time after Mother's first mastectomy when she seemed to be in remission for several months. She never hit Toni again.

The only time I remember Daddy hitting Toni was when he tried to help her with her algebra, and she just wasn't getting it. I think Daddy thought she was playing dumb, since I was listening, and even I understood. It only made Toni angrier that I thought I was smarter than she was.

After Mother died, Toni and I made peace. For a while we came to depend on each other. I needed to know where she was at all times, and she was kind to me the way she had been when she was in first grade. When Daddy had his heart attack a year almost to the day after Mother died, the family decided that I needed to go to live with my brother Ronald and his wife in Washington, DC. The doctors didn't think Daddy would survive.

We hadn't learned yet as a family to say I love you. It took my brother Bobby's wife, Yvonne, to teach us to hug each other when we met or parted, and say kind things to each other. I was scared. My whole idea of family had fallen away. I had grown up with a full house of family, but now our numbers had diminished every year. Not only would I be going to a new school, with all new people, it would be my first time going to an integrated school. Ronald assured us that the schools in DC had made the adjustment, and that people from all over the world went to the school I would attend.

The night before I left Petersburg, Toni didn't come to wish me well, or say she would miss me. She came to say, "You think you're so smart. You'll find out now that you're not." My days of wanting to be like my big sister were over. We didn't know how else to say, "I love you."

I excelled in school in DC in spite of the missing pieces in my early education. I had no background in science or foreign language. It wasn't that we didn't have a science class in Petersburg; we did. The science teachers I had, had other subjects as their primary responsibility -- Home Economics, or Auto Mechanics, and they did their best with the science classes that had been thrust upon them. We read the chapters and answered the questions at the end of the chapter. We didn't have laboratory equipment until black people started trying to integrate the schools, and the School Board tried to appease us with lab equipment and musical instruments. Any black person who might have enough expertise in science, would be teaching in a college, or would have left Petersburg to become a real scientist. My brother Ronald, who worked as a physicist for the Federal Department of Standards, had taught himself physics at Peabody High School in Petersburg.

When I graduated from Calvin Coolidge High School, Toni should have been graduating from Virginia State but she needed another twenty-some hours to finish. All of her close friends had graduated. Even her long-term boyfriend, Franklin, had left to take a job in Rochester, NY, writing to Toni that she wasn't what he needed in a wife. So rather than go to summer school, Toni thought she would seek her fortune in Washington. There were many of us Gordons there already. My brother George and his wife Shirley had settled there. Ronald and his wife Vivian owned a restaurant on Georgia Ave that they were trying to turn into a jazz club at night and cafeteria in the daytime, in addition to holding "day jobs" working for the Federal Government. My brother Michael was helping out for the summer between the terms when he taught school and Toni joined in as a waitress. By the end of the summer, Toni was pregnant, charmed by Trevor who was a student at Howard University, and from British Guiana. I was back in Virginia, preparing for my freshman year in college. While the world was focused on Dr. Martin Luther King and the March on Washington, I was packing for college, and Toni was planning an elopement.

Daddy had left the rectorate of St. Stephen's church in Petersburg some eight years before. His pastoral responsibility was on a circuit serving three small churches. Mother was still living when he started that phase of his ministry, but she insisted that we continue to live in Petersburg so her children could get a college education. Living in Petersburg had made it easy for my brothers and Toni to attend Va. State.

When Daddy was on the circuit, Toni had recently gotten

her driver's license, and jumped at the opportunity to drive Daddy to his churches in towns along the old US 301 corridor, Lawrenceville, Blackstone, and Kenbridge. Daddy and Toni became close in those days. Even with the influence of Yvonne, Daddy still didn't know how to say I love you. Still, he was the parent in the background to catch us when we fell. By the time Toni gave birth, Daddy knew she needed help, and told her to come home with that baby, Charles Armando Roberto Richards. Toni called him Junior, Junie, Junie Baruni. Daddy made sure she had the proper well-baby care, food and clothing. He even had the well-water tested to make sure it wouldn't harm Baruni. Daddy, who always used to say, "What would people say?" if we wanted to go to the movies on Sunday, didn't worry about what people would say when it came to Toni and that baby.

Toni later moved back to DC with her husband, but the marriage fell apart. Baruni was her pride and joy, and she did everything she knew how to, to give him the best. It seemed to me that Toni never got her self-esteem back. I always thought she lost her health because she didn't care enough about herself, but in those last years she found peace. Baruni, now Chuck, is a fine young man that any parent would be proud of.

When Toni's health started to fail in the 1990's it took years before her illness was diagnosed as Parkinson's disease. After she continued to lose mobility, and she retired on disability, Chuck made sure his Mom could stay in touch with the world by computer. Once she discovered that my job kept me accessible by email most of the day, we forged a new bond. If she had a question about how to do something on the computer, she sent me an email, and if I didn't answer quickly enough, she would call me at work. Toni was excited about my involvement in the Year 2000 system conversions, but she didn't live to see it happen.

Mother's song

Sometimes I feel like a Motherless child
A long way from home.
                    Negro Spiritual

Mother died when I was twelve years old. She died of breast cancer after four years of being in and out of the hospital, for double mastectomies, and radiation therapy. Chemotherapy wasn't widely available back then. She struggled to keep her job teaching at Disputanta Training School, but after so many absences they just didn't renew her contract.

I remember when she would disappear for long doctors' appointments. Nobody told me when she left the house, and I was very frustrated and lonely without her. After a while the loneliness was my normal state. Since I wasn't one to get into trouble, and did well in school, everybody thought I was fine. I was just very good at coping. I was left to my own devices and garnered my sense of morality from what my friends said their parents told them, or from what I read in the books that were my constant companions. I was raising myself.

In sixth grade, the boys and girls were split up for one period each day. The boys had Shop, and the girls had Home Economics, which became de facto Sex Education. One day early in the year, we had the "What Every Girl Should Know" tape sponsored by Modess sanitary pads. For some of the girls in my class, it was old news, since they already had their periods. It was news to me. The film showed diagrams of female anatomy, and talked about hygiene using the Modess belt and pads. The teacher gave us a booklet to take home to discuss with our mothers. When I showed mine to Mother, she thought it was very interesting, and brought out a similar book for me to read. It was the same information from Kimberly-Clark. The real sex education came later in Home Ec. class while we were doing our sewing assignments.

All the sixth grade girls had to make cotton skirts that year. The teacher told us how much fabric to buy, and she gave us instructions to cut the material without using a pattern. We learned how to use Singer Sewing machines operated by treadles. It was tricky getting that thing rocking in the right direction, and keeping it going at the right speed so we could sew the long seams of the skirt. The remainder of the skirt, putting in the waistband, and hemming, was done by hand. This became the time when we could talk while we worked.

There were several seventh-graders in the class who always wanted to talk about the stories they read in "True Confessions

Magazine." Sometimes they told the whole story, and if someone else had read that same edition, they would chime in with more details they remembered. Most of the stories were about girls who fell in love with the wrong boy and got pregnant. Some had illegal abortions or suffered some abuse by the boyfriend or their own family. I had never seen a True Confessions magazine, and I asked my friend Alice if she had. Alice was more worldly than I was, and she told me she had a collection of old True Confession magazines, that she had to hide from her mother. She told me I could come over and borrow some if I liked. After school that day, since I usually walked past Alice's house anyway when we walked home together, I stopped in and saw her collection. She also had copies of "Bronze Thrills" which had pictures of Negro women in their confession stories. I took a few magazines home and showed Mother. I was rather excited about my new find, and I knew my parents were not as conservative about such things as the parents of my friends. Mother even encouraged me to read them; she said I might learn something from those stories. Her encouragement made the books seem more like an assignment and took the excitement out of it. Still I read those books from Alice, and returned them to her.

Mother became concerned the next year, when Lynne had her first period, and I, at twelve, hadn't had mine. She sent me to the doctor who said I was fine, and that some girls develop later. Looking back, I think maybe she was trying to wrap up that loose end for me before she died that same year. Mother on her own decided to buy me a bottle of Lydia Pinkham's Compound that supposedly fixed all kinds of "female problems." It just made me gag. I secretly poured out a little every day so Mother would think I was taking it. When I finally did get my period, it was a month after Mother died, and Lynne had to let me borrow some supplies, and show me how to adjust the sanitary belt.

Most of the times Mother was in the hospital, I was too young to go to visit her. They didn't allow children under twelve at Petersburg General, but sometimes Daddy would take me to the parking lot where I could see Mother through the window, and she would wave to me. The time she was a patient at the Medical College in Richmond, they were a lot more lax about visitors, so Daddy took me along to visit. She was going through radiation at that time. She complained that her skin just burned so. Then she would take one of my cold hands (my hands have always been cold) and place it on her scarred chest to cool the burning. After a few minutes, my hand warmed up, and she would swap it for the other hand that was still cold. I would smile at her, knowing this was one thing I could do for her.

Mother instilled pride in all of us, but there were times

when we thought it was a hardship to walk instead of ride in the back of the bus. She wouldn't let us drink from the "colored only" fountains either. She said if we were so thirsty we could just walk home, the double whammy. When my friend Alice invited me to come with her to the public library, it didn't occur to me that Mother wouldn't approve. I went after school with Alice without asking. When Alice told me that we had to enter through the basement, and then I saw the piles of torn and worn out books, I knew I didn't want to be there.

Alice introduced me to the Librarian of the Colored Annex as it was called. Mrs. Elnora was a Filipino lady who sat at a desk in the basement. Alice bragged that Mrs. Elnora allowed her to take out books from the main library, and she would probably let me do the same. Mrs. Elnora explained that first I would have to take out books from the Annex, and once I showed that I could bring them back on time and in the same condition, then she would put me on the list to have access to the books upstairs. She said I could never go upstairs, but that she would bring the books downstairs for me. I decided on one book that didn't seem as battered as some of the others, but it was still in worse condition than any I had seen in our school library or than any of our books at home.

When I showed the book to Mother, explaining how I had gone to the Petersburg Library with Alice, Mother was furious.

"You will take that book back tomorrow. Who do they think they are that you have to get approval to use the public library? If we can't go first class, we don't go at all. If there is any book you want, you can get it from Giles B. Cook's library, or from Peabody High School. If they don't have what you want, your brothers can get anything you need from Virginia State."

I was stunned, but the next day, I took the book back. When I told Mrs. Elnora what Mother had said, she gave me a look that said, "You think you're too good to go to the Colored Annex." And in that moment I got it, and thought, "Yes!"

Mother was the task master. We had to be busy doing something, or she would find something for us to do. She insisted that we take pride in whatever task we had to do. One of my jobs was dusting the furniture in the front hall, living room and dining room. That included dusting off her collection of figurines on the what-not shelf in the living room, the draped lamp shades, the keys on the piano, and the carved wood base under the mahogany dining room table. It usually took an hour to do it by myself. When Lynne came to live with us, we shared that job. Then Mother would ask who did the best job. I shrugged, while Lynne said immediately that she did. Then I got a lecture about being proud of what I did, and if I couldn't be proud, maybe I needed something else to dust.

Mother's Song

If I had a task that I had chosen for myself, and was busy with it, Mother would let me go on doing it. I had a notebook for the poems that I wrote from the time I could write. When the notebook disappeared one day, I turned the house upside down looking for it, until Mother told me she had sent it to Simon & Schuster, the publisher. She told me she thought they could make my poems into a book. My heart soared at the thought of it, and quickly made myself another book of folded loose-leaf paper to start working on my next poems. I busied myself with thoughts of a book with my name on the cover, until the letter came from Simon & Schuster. Daddy always went outside to meet the mailman when he came down the street, so he was the first to see the large brown envelope with the Simon & Schuster return address. He gave it to me, and since it was addressed to Mother, I ran to her room for her to open it. They had returned my notebook with a letter. It was such a short letter, that she only had to glance over it quickly to tell me the bad news. She said she would keep my notebook, in case somebody else wanted to publish it. By that time, I had gotten in the habit of writing something every day, and I didn't give it up. Besides, Mother cherished my poems.

Most weekdays, Daddy cooked dinner. He had a regular schedule for what he would cook, so we knew that if it was Thursday, it was fried chicken. Friday was fish, and Saturday was preparation for Sunday. Mother would sometimes cook on Saturday, and she would give out assignments to me and Toni. By the time LaVerne and Lynne came back home, the kitchen would be buzzing with all of us on Saturday, if Mother felt well enough.

When Mother was busy at the sink washing vegetables, or at the table stirring up something, she would sing. Her song was always the same, "Sometimes I feel like a Motherless child, a long way from home." She would sing softly to herself, moaning and swaying.

I never heard first-hand the stories of my grandmother and her Mother. These became the stuff of family reunions after Mother died, when I learned that my grandmother, Mattie had lost her mother in childbirth. Mattie had been raised by a series of stepmothers who never treated her as part of the family. There was so much pain wrapped up in that one song, the pain of not being wanted, and pain of never knowing you're loved. I came to take it as an omen that since I also lost my mother, the same as all the women in my family line, that I was destined to continue the line of motherless children.

They didn't let me mourn. The day Mother died, Daddy came home from the hospital with her things. I was outside hanging wash on the line and saw him carrying her train case from the car.

Mother's Song

"Why are you bringing Mother's things? Where is she?"

"Mother won't be coming home." He seemed sad, but he continued on into the house without giving me any further explanation.

I said, "Oh," taking Daddy to mean she wouldn't be coming *today*, when he meant *ever*. I continued hanging my clothes on the line, when I heard Toni scream. She came running outside to get me, "What's the matter with you? Don't you know Mother is dead?!" I don't know if I fainted or just dissolved. It was not something I could comprehend. I was only twelve years old, still a "little girl," too young even to be allowed to visit in the hospital.

I easily dissolved into tears those days. I don't remember much of the days that followed. There were people coming and going who talked to Daddy and LaVerne, and my brothers. None of my friends came. Children didn't do condolences in those days. They had never told me that she would die. I had known there were surgeries, serious cutting and burning of her chest and armpits so there was hardly any muscle left to her arms, but death was beyond my understanding.

I cried until my pillow was wet on both sides, and my eyes were swollen shut. Michael decided we could play games and set up a card table in the living room. LaVerne thought it was disrespectful, since people were coming and going so much through the living room.

"But this is the first time she's stopped crying."

It was a little easier for that day. Then they brought her body to the house for the wake. I didn't find out until years later that it had been Mother's request to come home for her final viewing. I was terrified of the body, and could not go near her. That night Mother came to me in a dream. It was so real, her talking to me. She seemed happy when she told me she was nearby, but THEY wouldn't let her come to get me. She told me she would always be there. Daddy wouldn't let me go to the funeral because I was so upset, and he just couldn't stand to watch me cry.

If I had grown up Baptist or AME, instead of Episcopalian, there would have been more chances to mourn -- Mother's Days when everybody remembered Mama, and sang those tear-jerking songs when people could let it out. We didn't celebrate Mother's Day as a church event so it wasn't an occasion that I had to dredge up the old pain. I kept it all in. For a long time, LaVerne couldn't sit through the whole service on Sunday mornings. She would be there for while, and leave when she was overcome with grief. I just kept it in.

It happened that first Mother's Day before Ralph and I married. I attended his church in Newark most Sundays, and that Mother's Day, I wore one of my few matching outfits, grey and yellow with yellow shoes and purse. When I walked in the church I knew immediately I had messed up. All the other women and girls were wearing white. Ralph had bought me a white orchid to wear, so at least I was conforming to that custom.

Of course by that time I had given birth myself, but nobody there knew except Ralph. The whole service focused on Mother. The hymns and anthems and gospel songs were all about Mother, and Ralph preached about Mother. It was all about how the memory of Mother would bring you back to the faith that you were brought up in. When they started the song tributes to Mother, all of the pain of losing Mother, and the pain of losing Teal came back to me. It was the first time I had cried uncontrollably since Mother died. People all assumed it was all from remembering my Mother whom they knew had died. I used every tissue I had, and people around me started handing me handkerchiefs.

At the end of the service I couldn't escape. I didn't have a car, I didn't know the bus route, and I had to wait for Ralph to take me back to his apartment. People came up to me to inquire if I was all right, and I mumbled something about my mother. Ralph hadn't even known that I had cried through half the service until he came up to me and saw my face, eyes all swollen and nose all red. He asked what was wrong, and I said, "I have to find my Teal."

He said, "You have to forget that."

I muffled my tears until I could get in the car, and I bawled the rest of the day until he took me for my train back to New York. He didn't want to talk about it. It was a closed subject as far as he was concerned. I needed to learn to control myself.

Those Clubs

When we were classmates in Mrs. Alice Vernon's second grade class at Giles B. Cooke elementary School in Petersburg, Virginia, Alice, Zelma, Yvonne, and I started the Walking Club. Every Sunday afternoon, we would walk around Petersburg in our Sunday best – crinoline skirts, patent leather shoes, and little white socks. We window shopped downtown on Sycamore Street, looked in the windows of Rucker-Rosenstock, and Woolworth's, and stopped for a treat at People's Drug Store on the corner of Washington St. Sometimes we went down to the train station and followed the tracks across train trestles, holding our breath, hoping a train wouldn't come. Or we might go to Pocahontas Park, play on the slides, and drink from the cold water fountain that didn't have a "For Colored" sign. We would end up at somebody's house, according to the schedule for whose turn it was, and have another dessert, while trying to conceal the dirt and occasional rips we had gotten in our clothes.

By the time we reached puberty, the walks were replaced by our interest in boys, and the activities we could find that included them. We were fast friends, until I moved away, sent to live with my brother after Mother died. I wrote letters, but nobody was as prolific a writer as I was. Besides, they still had each other there in Petersburg. We saw each other on holidays and during the summer, but we never recaptured that time when we were all the same height. Alice is still 4'11", but I became the tallest at 5'6."

In 1995, the year we all turned fifty, I started talking to Yvonne about getting together to celebrate our birthdays. Yvonne was the only one of us who still lived in Petersburg, and kept in touch with everybody, since we always knew where to find her. And so was launched our first reunion.

What did four fifty-year-old women talk about? I had lost touch with Alice and Zelma, and there was so much to catch up with – marriages, children, divorces, separations, deaths of parents. Zelma showed us photos of her five-year-old son and two-year-old granddaughter. We all agreed that we looked the same, and we looked good, even with twenty to thirty extra pounds each, except for Alice, who was still the same size.

When we parted we promised to stay in touch and have another reunion soon. Alice and I kept in touch more. She and her husband stopped through Raleigh, and I visited her in the Washington, DC area. It had been easy to visit back and forth with Yvonne and her husband, since my sister still lived in Petersburg. Then when the CIAA Basketball tournament came to

Those Clubs

Raleigh for a five-year term, I became their host for CIAA week each year.

When we came to our 60th year, we came together again. And what did we talk about? All the transitions of age – more deaths of parents and siblings, eldercare, the blessings of grand-children. And we still looked good. We all agreed how blessed we are to still have our health and sound minds. We spent time remembering those who had passed – classmates, teachers, my husband. And we praised God for what we had come through, remarking how we didn't accept the relationships that our moth-ers put up with. Yvonne was divorced. Alice and her husband had retired and moved back to Petersburg, where they started a church.

I told them how my youngest son asked on that first reunion if all my school friends were light-skinned. My response had been, "I really hadn't noticed that before." There were so many fair-skinned blacks in Petersburg when we grew up that we didn't pay a lot of attention to skin color, since the white people called us all "Colored" anyway. Somebody mentioned Alvin, whose cancer had returned, Alvin who was whiter than most white people in town, Alvin who had married a white girl he met in college, and never looked back.

This time when we parted we talked of getting together more – a cruise, the MEAC tournament in Raleigh, a trip to

Pennsylvania, and we promised not to wait another 10 years. We might not live to see it.

*   *   *

My friends in Petersburg remain my lifelong friends, but it is not the same way with my friends from Washington DC. It's a wonder I survived those years reasonably intact, after losing and never being allowed to mourn the loss of Mother, then being thrown into the Washington DC world of class and caste.

My brother Ronald and his wife Vivian did the best they could with me. They both worked long hours, departing for work before I went off to school, leaving baby Ronnie with a woman who came in every day. I was the babysitter's relief when I came home after school, taking care of Ronnie until they came home from work. This arrangement worked until I reached high school, and I wanted to participate in after school activities. Then they had the sitter to stay later. Vivian thought I needed more social development, since I hadn't had dance lessons or any participation in organizations such as Jack and Jill that were meant to develop young ladies and gentlemen. She found a class at the Y to teach me makeup, style, how to walk and how to dress. I thought I had my own style by then, but I did go along with the class since it also included a one-hour fencing lesson every week. Even after I "graduated" from that finishing class, I asked Vivian if I could take more fencing lessons, since I enjoyed the strenuous workout.

Ronald made sure the school system recognized my good grades and advanced subjects that placed me in the Honors Track. That didn't seem like such a big deal until I found that there were only two other blacks in the Honors Track at Paul Jr. High School that year, Adele who was in my homeroom, and Kenny.

Adele showed me around that year, without getting very close. One day we were standing outside after lunch and a boy came our way and pointed to Adele, saying "ABCD." When I asked Adele what he was talking about, she explained that they had been a club, Adele, Barbara, Camilla, and Diane. They had been in school together since elementary school. She didn't say anything further about them but I could see it in the way they hardly even spoke to each other on the school yard that Adele was not included in their activities anymore. I met them later in the lunch room, and Camilla checked me out, saying, "Nice hair." They took note of the fact that I was in the Honors Track with Adele. I thought I could see what the friction with Adele was all about. She was in, they were not. Camilla went further in vetting me, and came over to see where I lived with Ronald and Vivian. "Nice house." And she seemed to be taking note of everything, how I was babysitting Ronnie after school, how I didn't have a real bedroom set, and that I was still living out of my suitcase at that time.

The BCD group invited me to some of their social events, the Youth Fellowship at their church, dances, and skating. Adele was never invited. I started to understand they were only including me to get back at Adele, for whatever it was that she had done to them.

Adele and I became closer. I helped her with math, and she helped me with English. I had never had a problem with English Composition before, but Mrs. Tolson didn't like anything I wrote. I would hang out at Adele's house after school, or she would be at mine. Ronald sized my new friends up by comparing them to the typical friends group that you see in cartoons and movies. There is always a fat bossy one, like Camilla, a pretty one like Adele, and I would be the smart one. Seeing them like that, just made me laugh about the whole situation, and not care about Camilla's agenda. The fact that Adele was prettier than the others probably contributed to whatever problem Camilla had with her. Adele was "pecan tan," with curly black hair down to her butt. All the boys knew her and she didn't hesitate to speak to everybody.

* * *

When we reached high school, Adele and I were closer friends. Her parents didn't allow her to date, and I was never asked out. Of course I had my boyfriend Mack in Petersburg, but I only saw him on holidays and in the summer. Our group of friends had grown to include Pamela, the sisters Nina and Connie, and Leila. It was Adele's idea to start a club. We played with different names for our group. Adele's first suggestion was "*les jeunes filles*," because French was her favorite subject in school, but the other girls thought the guys from St. John's School who had a club called "*les jeunes hommes*" would think that we were trying to get with them, or set ourselves up as their sister-club without their approval. So we decided on "The Ingénues." Adele was our first club president.

The whole purpose of a high school club was to identify us as friends. Sometimes we would dress alike, or sit together at lunch, which wasn't always possible with our different schedules. Adele, Pamela, and I hung out together the most, and we would spend time at Pamela's house since she lived about halfway between me and Adele. None of us had a real boyfriend, except I still had Mack back in Petersburg, my summer and holiday boyfriend.

Then along came Warren. We were juniors by then, and Warren was a senior. Pamela confided in me that she had spotted him in the cast of the spring production of "Guys and Dolls," and was conveniently placing herself outside of rehearsal and his math class every day so she would run into him. Adele confided in me that somebody had given Warren her phone number and he had called her several times. I was caught in the middle and couldn't tell either of them that the other had a "thing" for Warren.

At first Adele didn't seem to care much about him, but she was enjoying the attention. Pamela was so smitten, I knew she would be hurt, so I told her before she did anything more to embarrass herself. And then I told Adele that Pamela had liked Warren, too. Pamela was great about it, backed off of Warren, and started stalking another guy. I could tell she was hurt because it seemed Adele could have her pick of any guy she wanted.

Adele's parents still didn't allow her to date. They clamped down even harder when we got to senior year and Adele became a cheerleader. Pamela had tried out, but didn't make the cut. There were only eight cheerleaders, and that was the first year that there was more than one black cheerleader. The other one was fair-skinned with sandy colored hair, so some people wouldn't have known she was black. By then Adele had cut her hair to shoulder length, and the boys were after her all the more.

I fell into the cheerleader's buddy role, hanging around like I had no life of my own, until my own extra-curricular activities took off. I had been on the yearbook staff in junior year, and became an assistant editor in senior year. Adele insisted that we go out for hockey, since the girls' hockey season fell between the big cheerleading seasons. We had to learn hockey rules in gym class, and since I had aced the written tests, I made the team. Our gym teacher/coach had once been an Olympic hockey player, and she insisted on our knowing the rules. So we were the team who played by the rules against other teams who won by brute force. We had a perfect season...lost every game.

By then Warren was in college at Howard University, but he would stop by Coolidge to see Adele. I was still always around, even with the two of them. That way if Adele's parents asked where she had been, she could truthfully say she was with Sarah. Warren teased me a lot, even tried to fix me up with one of his "boys," but it never worked. Since I played "Left Inner" position in hockey, he liked to tease me, calling me "Left Out."

I didn't feel like I was being used, but it all came to a head after we went to see the movie "Phaedra" with Melina Mercouri and Anthony Perkins. It was an assignment for Warren's literature class, and I loved the movie anyway. Adele and Warren whispered together in French all through the movie. They often did that, since Adele had had four years of French and Warren was struggling with college French, and they knew I wouldn't understand their conversation. Adele had told her parents she was going to the movie with me, as we had done for years. This time, Warren drove his mother's car, and dropped me off at home after the movie.

The next day I got a call from Adele's mother. Adele didn't come home after the movie. I had to confess that we had been with Warren, and they had dropped me off after the movie. So they sent the police to come to talk to me. I told them what I knew, and that I didn't think she was in any danger. Warren wouldn't hurt her, and I knew she had her period, so they probably wouldn't have sex. I didn't know they were planning anything because they had been talking in French. They asked the same questions over and over, probably to see if I changed my story, and to make sure I didn't leave something out.

My sister-in-law, Vivian was furious with Adele for leaving me holding the bag. "She just used you. She's no friend of yours. And you need to put her out of the club." Vivian was more upset than I was. I didn't tell anybody that Adele had confided in me about her nighttime visits from Warren on the fire escape outside her bedroom window. I should have known they were heading down a dangerous path, but Warren was a "good" boy. He called me "lame" but he was as much of a wimp as I was. And he was thoroughly infatuated with Adele.

They came back two days later. They had spent the time driving and driving, all the way to Ohio and back. They didn't have much money on them; it wasn't planned. After that Adele was on lock-down, and I never heard what Warren's parents had to say to him.

Vivian insisted I tell the rest of the club what had happened. Rumors were flying all over the school, but I had not told anything to anybody. The club met. I was President by that time. Vivian was our advisor, and she told the girls what she thought. So we suspended Adele from the club for several months, but the club was never the same, and neither was our friendship after that. Adele and I still talked a lot, but we didn't go out anywhere together the way we once did.

By that time we were waiting to hear from colleges about admissions and scholarships. I applied to Penn State, Syracuse, and Drew. In those days we were advised to apply to only the schools we were serious about. Ronald had made sure I sent for catalogs from the schools he considered the best for math and science, Rensselaer and MIT, and he was disappointed that I didn't apply to them. They seemed much bigger than Drew and Syracuse, where I thought I would be more comfortable. I had learned about those schools from catalogs, and recommendations from the National Scholarship Service and Fund for Negro Students. Drew in particular didn't have any Negro Students, and NSSFNS thought I should do the right thing by going. I was accepted to all three schools. Penn State didn't have money for scholarships for out of state students. Syracuse and Drew both offered scholarships.

At the weekly assembly at Coolidge, college acceptances and scholarships were announced, and I had my time to stand and be recognized several times. The school counselor, who announced the awards, still expected Sarah Gordon to be one of the Jewish students. All the other Gordons at Coolidge were Jewish. You would think that he would stop being surprised when I stood. He had been no help at all in advising me for college. I had met with him only once, and he was surprised that time. Even while looking at my grades and SAT scores, he said since I didn't have any money for college, I should apply to DC Teachers College. I never went back to see him.

Adele applied to Michigan State and Kalamazoo. She wanted to get as far away from home as possible. Pamela's family was moving to California, so she opted for California schools. After graduation, Ronald and Vivian were moving to California as well, and I would go back to Virginia to spend the summer preparing for college. My friends and I said our goodbyes as if we would see each other again in a few days. We wrote for a little while. Again, I was more the writer than they were. And then we lost track of each other.

Years later, after I married Ed, I found that his sister-in-law lived across the street from Adele's house. The sister-in-law had moved there the year after Adele and I had graduated from Coolidge. She didn't know the family, but vaguely remembered the

66

daughter had been very sick. The last letter I had from Adele, she had come back from Kalamazoo because of some heavy bleeding episodes, and she had become too weak to live in the dorm. I later found her on the internet listed with the missing alumni for the class of 1967 of Kalamazoo College.

Special Teachers

You wouldn't think that a band director would have such an impact on my life, especially since he taught me only a few weeks in the summer. It was the summer of 1958, and in September, I would be starting eighth grade, the first year of high school at Peabody High. My sister Toni decided that I should join the band. Toni was a "rising senior" and had been a member of the marching band for all of her years in high school. Toni had signed up for band class in summer school, and she told me that she would get permission from the band director, Mr. Hayes so that I could come too. Since we were always on the lookout for summer activities, I decided that band class would be like going to camp.

When Toni introduced me to Mr. Hayes, he was happy to have me in band. Toni was one of his favorite students, since she played in the marching band, the concert band, and the jazz combo. Toni's instrument was the alto saxophone, but she could also play clarinet. She had stuck with piano lessons longer than I had, and she played well enough to participate in concerts. My brother George had also played in the Peabody band when he came along. We never owned an instrument in the family aside from the piano, and would depend upon the instruments supplied by the school. Since Toni had standing as a member of the band, she was assigned a saxophone at the beginning of the school year, and it was hers to take home for practice. I hadn't thought about what instrument I would play, but Mr. Hayes had already decided that it should be the flute, since he had just received several new instruments including one flute.

The beginning band class was in the morning session before the temperature in the school rose above eighty-five degrees, in those days before central air-conditioning. During the two hours, Mr. Hayes gave personal attention to the new students like me who had never held their instruments before. We had time for marching drills and formations on days when it was not too hot, and we always ended the day playing all together as a band. At first we played just the scales, while we learned to follow Mr. Hayes as conductor.

At the end of the first class, Mr. Hayes said I could take the flute home to practice my scales. I was pleased to be doing something new, and determined to practice more consistently than I had with the piano when I was four years old. By the second day, I had learned my scales well, and could follow the music in the book. But at the end of the day, Mr. Hayes told me that I had to share the instrument with another girl who was in the afternoon class. He set up a schedule for us to take turns taking the flute home. When it was my turn to take it home, I would have to come back at two o'clock after the second session to pick it up when the other girl had finished her class.

Mr. Hayes showed me how I could practice without an instrument. He said if I remembered my fingering and followed the notes in the music, I would be able to hear the music in my head. I gave him a doubting stare, but I said I would try it. I found that on days when I didn't have the instrument, I would concentrate harder when I practiced, and on the next day at school, Mr. Hayes would be pleased at how I had improved more when I was only visualizing the flute.

One afternoon when I had to come back at two to get the flute to take home, I overheard Mr. Hayes talking to another teacher as I was coming in the room. Those words stuck with me for the rest of my life. I heard him say, "If Sarah tells you she's going to do something, you can count on it." It seemed such a natural thing to always live up to my word, that I was surprised that anyone would make mention of it. After hearing Mr. Hayes praise me that way, I felt I had to live up to his opinion of me. I enjoyed that summer in the band, but I didn't continue with the flute after Mother died that September.

*   *   *

The most important teacher in my life was my eighth grade algebra teacher, who happened to be my sister LaVerne.

LaVerne had moved back home after her divorce, and she and her daughter Lynne lived with us all on West Street. Most of the time I could keep my teacher LaVerne and my sister LaVerne in separate compartments. My friends, however, never let me forget that the teacher was my sister, and would create weird scenarios by coming to the house hoping to sneak a peak when LaVerne was preparing a big test. They would even try to bribe me to get a copy of the test beforehand. It didn't occur to me to cheat, since math was my best subject, and making 100's was a challenge I enjoyed.

It was a few years after the Supreme Court decision in Brown v. Board of Education struck down the concept of "Separate but Equal" in public schools. The schools in the South were dragging their feet when it came to integration, and several black communities would put forward a Negro student or a few, to request admission to their local white school.

This was part of the impetus at Peabody High to create an advanced group of students. We didn't otherwise have tracks for students. Everybody was thrown in together, and the brighter students might sometimes be held back by the slower ones, with the curriculum being geared for someone in the middle. They created a group, eight of us who would start algebra in the eighth grade, so we would be ready for calculus and physics before graduation. I suspected that they were also trying to groom someone to integrate the white school.

Years later when LaVerne remembered that class with the eight of us eighth graders thrown in with ninth grade algebra, she said it was a special class. There were many of us who were compulsive achievers, who thrived under LaVerne's style of teaching. She gave us a syllabus like college students might have, listing the all the assignments for the six-week grading period. We were required to do all our class work and homework in a spiral-bound notebook which she would check, walking around the class while we did class work. I think it was Alice, my friend from the walking club, who first decided to do assignments in advance of when they were due, and before we knew it, half the class was racing to keep up with her. Alice and I had had a friendly competition since second grade, and we always helped each other along. When we both got stuck doing work in advance of when it was taught in class, LaVerne might give us tips in her walk around the room, so we could keep going further. If it was going to require more than a few tips, we would just have to wait until it was taught according to the schedule. Most of us finished all the assigned work well before the end of the grading period, so LaVerne would have to give us some bonus problems to do.

It was in the months after Mother died, and when my name came up in the discussion of integration, Daddy declined for me.

I had been through too much already, just losing my Mother. The evening news was full of the integration incidents in other Southern states, showing how the single Negro child, or maybe a group of two or three would be harassed, spit upon, and pelted with tomatoes or eggs. Daddy couldn't allow that to happen to me. Eventually the committee decided on a boy from our group to be "The One."

By the following September, Daddy became very sick, and was hospitalized after a massive heart attack. The doctors didn't expect him to make it, and called all of us children together. Even Bobby came home from Germany. Toni and I were the only children left at home, and Toni was starting her freshman year at Virginia State. She would be in town, but she could live in the dorm. Daddy's last worry was me. It was then that my siblings decided that I should go to live with Ronald and his wife Vivian. They lived in Washington, DC, and were expecting their first child.

They put the question to me to decide, weighing the pros and cons. I would be going to an integrated school after all. I would have my own room for the first time in my life. Ronald and Vivian didn't have a working TV, but Michael said we could take his. Ronald and Vivian would have me as a built-in baby-sitter. Did I have a choice in the matter? The doctors didn't expect Daddy to make it, and having a teenager around might push him over the edge that much faster. My brother George's girlfriend Shirley, who had been like part of the family for as long as I could remember, let me borrow one of her suitcases, and I had everything packed to go in a few days.

When I look back on that day, I can see all of my siblings together, each bringing his or her input to the problem. Even though I was the problem, I can see myself now as the center of that old orchestra song, and all of us singing in tune. I couldn't see it then as the love we have for each other, but I see it now.

There were only two other Negro students in my classes when Ronald enrolled me at Paul Junior High School that year. That didn't bother me as much as having all white teachers. My homeroom teacher was Mrs. Perkins who also taught algebra. Since I had already had algebra I and there was no higher level math at Paul JHS, there I was repeating it. The counselor probably thought I might need repeating it anyway since I came from a segregated school system. Mrs. Perkins set out to challenge my ability by calling on me to do problems on the board every time she could, until she was satisfied that I could do them. She stopped calling on me to do problems, but I was always in her face with my hand up.

English class was a different matter. While I had always gotten good grades in English and especially English composition, Mrs. Tolson seemed to hate everything I wrote. She corrected my "choice of language," on words like "nauseated" which she corrected as "nauseous." Apparently there was some standard form for composition that everybody learned in seventh and eighth grade Honors English that I didn't know about. Mrs. Tolson asked me where my theme sentence was and various other things I didn't understand. When I asked her after class she wouldn't have time and started talking about moving me to the appropriate track. Luckily Adele stepped in and volunteered to show me the ropes. Once I had the formula right, I still couldn't please Mrs. Tolson, who gave me C's on everything I wrote.

And there were the cursed sentence diagrams. We had had only a minimal amount of sentence diagramming in Petersburg; only a few of us in my class could get the subject – predicate – object of a preposition right, but we had never diagrammed subordinate clauses, and the subjunctive mode. For the first time in my life, I was the "slow one" in class.

That was the same year many public school systems in Virginia refused to comply with Brown v. Board of Education. Rather than wait to see if a Negro student would seek admission to one of the white schools, they shut down the schools and the white people withheld their property taxes to funnel them into "Christian" schools that would be all white. That didn't happen in Petersburg, but it was happening all around. It was no secret at Paul Junior High that I had come from Virginia, and was living with my brother. Ronald had enrolled me in the school, and both he and Vivian attended the Parent-Teacher conferences. One of the teachers asked if my school system back home had been shut down. I told her no, I had come to live with my brother because my mother had died.

There were reports in the Washington Post that the DC Public Schools were seeing an influx of children from Virginia. Soon after that I received a letter to take home explaining that since I was not a resident of the District of Columbia, I would have to pay tuition to attend the schools there. Ronald responded with a letter the next day that he was my guardian, and that I was a resident of DC. Then the letters and calls went back and forth with Ronald insisting, and the school asking for documentation of his guardianship. Of course there was no documentation. Daddy had not officially given up being my parent. Then in the midst of all the back and forth, one day in December, I was called to the office at school and told I would have to leave, turn in all my books, clean out my locker, goodbye.

It was a shock. I remember walking around in a daze, taking my things, and carrying my books around to all my teachers with a form for them to check off. I didn't believe what was happening. I had to interrupt most of my teachers during their class to get their signature. They couldn't stop to talk to me. I caught my Ancient History teacher between classes, and she asked, "Where will you go?"

I was starting to tear up, and said, "I don't know."

She squeezed my hand, "Good luck."

When Ronald came home from work he assured me I would be back in school before long, and not to worry. He had already prepared his case to present to the House Committee for the District, since DC had no home rule at the time, and what would have been School Board decisions were being made by Congressmen from places all over the country. We treated it like an exciting exercise in Civics. Ronald showed me all the papers he was going to present, and we all went to the Committee hearing before Congress broke for Christmas. I don't know who was on the committee at the time, but it seemed that there were a bunch of white Southern men, deciding my fate. They listened politely, and decided quickly, "No" I would have to pay tuition. Tuition at the time was about $150 per semester. That may not seem like a lot of money, but it was more than any of my brothers had paid in tuition to attend Virginia State College.

When I finally got back to school, it was January. My teachers had been instructed to exclude the missing weeks from my record, and I would jump into the work without having to make up any assignments. I would have to figure out how to catch up on my own. The only class where I had an issue was music. Since I had been in the Glee Club, I was exempt from taking exams in music class. The grading was pass/fail anyway, and Glee Club required a lot of additional time due to rehearsals before and after school and performances at school and around the city. The music teacher wasn't expected to hold my absence against me, but at my first rehearsal on returning, she singled me out to listen to my voice, told me I didn't know the part, and would have to take the exam for the grading period...THAT DAY.

The exam was to write the number of sharps or flats for each key, A-sharp through G-flat. She gave me 10 minutes to look at my notes if I had any. I had paid attention in music even though I hadn't been required to take the tests, and I managed to pull out of somewhere the correct answers for every key. I aced her little exam. Then she told me that I had done better than all the students who had been there for every class. She allowed me to continue to be in the Glee Club, but I would have to lip-synch for the next performance. That was a performance I didn't want to miss, since we would sing at the White House. They sang; I lip-synched. But I was there. President Eisenhower was out of town. But I was there.

High school was a relief. I was still in Honors, but since there were more black students in Honors, there was less of a stigma attached to it. In addition, since we could take a variety of elective courses that did not have an Honors component, there was less of an issue of who was in honors. I was in English with my same friends from Paul, the 10th grade English Honors class taught by Mrs. Good. Her focus was on composition and literature. All the old composition rules flew out the window, and I was free to express myself the way I had done before Mrs. Tolson. Mrs. Good enjoyed my different "choice of language" and liked my style. My classmates were surprised when the "slow one" was getting A's in composition, while their formula-based essays sometimes earned C's. My self esteem took a real leap that year with Mrs. Good.

She was an overweight and cuddly woman who had a gleam in her eye when she greeted us and whenever she got excited about some point of English composition or grammar. Every time she handed back our composition assignments she would write eight to ten sentences on the board from our work, sentences that had typical errors and we could benefit from correcting together. They were dangling modifiers, lack of parallelism, subject/verb disagreement or vague descriptions. When we finally "got it," oh how she gleamed.

At some point, Mrs. Good started using an outside Reader to grade some of our composition work. It was intended to relieve her of some of the work of grading papers, but in reality she read all of our work just the same. It was also expected to give us more unbiased grades, since the Reader had never seen any of us, and didn't have a history of liking or disliking anybody's writing. I still made A's in composition with an occasional B, which Mrs. Good would review afterwards.

That was the year Mrs. Good decided that we should enter the National Scholastic Writing contest. Every student was assigned to write a short story according to the contest rules, the prescribed length, typed double-spaced with 1 inch margins, minimum of 10 pages. Mrs. Good gave us copies of past winning stories so we would know what the judges liked. We had two weeks to deliver our first draft, typed in the format for the contest. Mrs. Good turned the whole batch over to the Reader to grade.

After my cry-baby days passed when I reached puberty, I developed a way of managing shock and total disappointment by going into slow reaction mode. The day Mrs. Good handed back our first draft, I could feel it coming by her body language, the way she was avoiding eye-contact with me, holding my paper for last. There it was, a big fat F. I could feel my eyes welling up with tears, and the students around me gasping. Nobody ever got an F in Honors English. Mrs. Good said to me quietly, that she would see me after class, and that it was not an F paper. Of course the other students quickly took up on it, and sought to talk to Mrs. Good after class about whatever grade they had, and when she gave me a knowing smile, I knew I could laugh about it with her later. She reminded the class that this was only the first draft, and she would choose the ten best stories to work with further. "Sarah's story is one of the ten."

After class she told me there was a problem with the Reader. The reason she had taken the job was that she had been an English teacher, but she wanted to work from home to be near her child who had a manic-depressive disorder. Apparently the child had often told her mother that she would kill her. My story was the true story of the days following my Mother's death, in which I went through the mourning, anger, guilt, confusion of losing a parent. In one point of my story, I had written, "Maybe Mother was better off dying." The Reader lost all objectivity at that point, and saw nothing but an F for my story. Mrs. Good told me this in confidence, because she did not want to undermine the usefulness of the independent reader program.

She continued to work with ten of us on our stories. This was extra work for us as well as for her, since we still had to keep up with the rest of our assignments in English. In those days, when all anybody had was a mechanical typewriter, carbon paper, and a good eraser, it took hours to produce a good typed copy for the contest. Mine still had some erasure marks, but I completed it, and submitted it for the contest. It was months later that the winners were announced. I received an honorable mention for the DC region. One other student at Coolidge, in another grade, did as well. Those were the only awards for the whole school for that contest. I was elated, I was vindicated. When the list was published in the Washington Post I found my name among the many columns of awards that were published for all the public schools in the District for the school semester. I wanted to cut it out and send it to Mrs. Tolson, and say, "So there."

Mrs. Good was a joy to all of the class that year, and when we reached senior year, she was our teacher again. It was the best time of the day to be in her class. She never got upset with anybody, except for that day in the spring of our senior year; when we had a bad case of Senioritis. We were laughing and giggling at the slightest thing, while evoking a memory of the previous night's Steve Allen Show by holding up "COMM'L" signs, the way Steve Allen did, when we needed a break from laughing. That day Mrs. Good just walked out abruptly, leaving all of us feeling guilty about our behavior.

Alan who was one of the co-editors of the school newspaper took charge. He was one who could be such a class clown one minute, and all serious and organized when it was necessary. He got us to working on some project that was coming due, and said we ought to write an apology to give Mrs. Good when she returned. We were quiet the rest of the period, and didn't see Mrs. Good again until the next day. When she started the class, Alan started to make a speech of apology, but she stopped him and said it was she who needed to apologize to us for walking out on us. It wasn't our foolish behavior at all, rather the bad news she had received just before class about the death of a friend that had upset her. We behaved better that day.

Mrs. Good was invited to the fortieth reunion of our class. She sent regards since she was no longer able to travel.

I ♥ NY

I suppose it was New York that got me through the years at Drew. That shining beacon by the sea, always there, sometimes mean, cruel, but always exciting. And even when she knocked me down, she was still there. And when she was knocked down, I was there watching, mourning.

My first trip to NY was on one of our family trips. Mother must have loved NY as much as I did later. She was the adventurer. I don't know why in the world she chose to go to NYU in the summer to take classes. I was still a pre-schooler when she went to summer school at Virginia State in Petersburg, trying to complete her Bachelors degree. And there was at least one summer that she took courses at New York University. On this particular family trip it was a few years after she had taken those courses.

I was eight years old, and there were seven of us on the trip, me, Lynne, Toni, Michael, George, Daddy and Mother. On these trips we would live mostly in the car. We bought groceries, ate by the roadside, and slept in the car. We traveled like that every summer. Some years we would go to visit Aunt Sarah in Forsythe, Georgia, and some years it seemed that we would follow a trail of Daddy's college and seminary classmates. I don't know if they knew he was going to show up with a car full of family, but they would take us in, and that was our vacation. There were few hotels where Negroes could stay in the south, not that we could have afforded it anyway.

When we got to New York, Mother and we girls stayed at a rooming house, the place where Mother had lived her summer at New York University. We had a room with a bed, a chair, and a desk, and the shared bathroom down the hall. Toni, Lynne, and I slept in the bed, and Mother slept in the chair. Daddy and the boys stayed at the YMCA. The accommodations were pretty awful, but it was so exciting to be in New York City. We walked the streets with our necks craned, looking up at the buildings that kissed the sky, and the neon lights that took our breath away. And it was so dirty, that every night we had to wash away the rings around our collars. We ate at the AUTOMAT, and went to Sunday service at the Cathedral of St. John the Divine.

I didn't see New York again until I went away to college at Drew University in Madison, New Jersey. It wasn't until I met Billy that I learned how close and how easy it would be to go to "The City." There were six Negro students in the whole college that year, all of us freshmen, three girls, three boys, a matched set, or so it seemed they had planned. The Dean of Women, an old Victorian-minded biddy, who had no tolerance for the mixing of races, managed to arrange the women in the dorm by ethnic groups.

I arrived early in the dorm that first day. The family had driven me up from Petersburg, and left to get back the same day. When my roommate, Gwen, arrived she was preceded by her mother and sister and SIX large red matching suitcases. I was relieved and surprised that she was also black. One of our friends in the dorm later told us that the survey we filled out for roommate preference had a check-box for, "I prefer not to have a Negro roommate." The forms that Gwen and I received said only "I prefer not to have a roommate who smokes." So it seemed to us the third black girl, Edna, found the only white girl who didn't mind rooming with a Negro. It made us a little angry, but after the first few days of talking well into the night, Gwen and I decided we were a good match, both preachers' kids from the south, both Math majors. We also observed that the good Dean of Women had also matched up the other "ethnic" types. For a couple of southern black girls, those folk were all white, but old Deanie-poo had put the Italians, the Greeks, the Irish, the Scottish all in their separate pigeon holes. There weren't any Asians, and the one Hispanic girl in the college was an upper-classman.

I Love NY

The "smoker" girls were all at the front of the floor. Not that they all smoked, but they didn't mind the smoke, and they seemed to be the more popular girls who had regular dates every weekend. The non-smokers tended to congregate together in the floor lounge when the smoker girls were out for the evening. Sometimes groups would gather in our room. Our next door neighbors were Binky who was Italian, and Gale who was Greek. Binky started coming to our room when her roommate wouldn't talk to her. Andrea, whom we called Andi, had a very strange roommate who was an art major. Her pen and ink drawings of demons and horned creatures frightened Andi so much that she often wound up in our room as well.

Freshman orientation was held at a camp in the woods of New Jersey for four days. We were instructed that we would be roughing it, and that the girls were not allowed to have make-up or hair curlers. The attire was to be jeans and shirts. We bunked in large cabins that held a dozen people each, including an orientation counselor for each cabin. This was to be a time of bonding for the freshman class before we were thrown into the mild hazing by the sophomores back on campus. Between the orientation meetings, the family style meals, and late-night chats in the cabins, I felt it was a place where I could belong. We were indoctrinated into the Liberal Arts education. Drew was a place where the whole person would be educated. The required courses for everyone included math, literature, a lab science, philosophy or religion, gym including a requirement to swim four laps of the pool. At the end of the days in the woods we were excited about returning to campus with all the new friends we had bonded with. The shock for Gwen and me when we got back to the dormitory was that the girls we knew at camp didn't know us anymore.

Gwen developed an ulcer that first year from the subtle racism we experience at Drew, mostly in the dorm. Gwen, who came from Birmingham, and had been one of the high school students who demonstrated with Martin Luther King, and had been fire-hosed, and had police dogs sicked on, couldn't deal with the questions like "How can you tell when you're dirty?" the looks that said, "You brush your teeth, too?" and the people who called us by the wrong name because "we all look alike." There were jerks who tried to start a conversation with one of us by saying, "Now which one are you?" The worst was having an instructor who insisted that Gwen was Edna, and that Gwen had to be lying, trying to cover up. Gwen was 5' 9" and built like a "brick house," while Edna was 5' 2" and rather round and plump. They were taking the same zoology course from the same instructor but at different times of day.

I had my own incident with a professor that upset me greatly when it happened, but I was able to chalk it off to her insensitivity and down-right meanness, so it didn't reflect on me at all. It happened in the first semester of economics when we were studying economic history. The topic of the day was slavery, and my professor asked the class "What were the economic advantages of slavery?" I was the only black person in the class, and the other students looked around. but nobody answered. So she called on me. Some of the guys in the class thought it was hilarious that she singled me out for that question. and looked at me and laughed out loud. I mumbled something. left the class and could hear them howling in the background. When I told my friend Neil about it, he thought I should try to be objective, and separate my own personal view of the pain of slavery from the facts that I recognized. Free slave labor was definitely an advantage to the development of this country. I tried to prepare my answer for a comeback, but the subject never came up again in class.

Most of our classmates were from Northern New Jersey, from suburban communities that had no blacks. Some of those communities had restrictive covenants that were later ruled illegal, that prevented people from selling their houses to blacks. In 1963 you rarely even saw a black person on TV, and many of our dorm mates down the hall confessed they had never before seen a black person "In Person."

One of the worst things about Drew was being invisible.

We couldn't participate in the rites of winter or spring, because we were not even there. At the first big snowfall, the guys would build a snow fortress and prepare an arsenal of snowballs to pelt the girls as they left the dining hall after dinner. The snow wasn't icy, so nobody got hurt. At least it looked like good fun. At least it did until Gwen or Edna or I walked by, and everything stopped. If somebody gave a signal, we didn't hear it. The same thing happened in the spring with the annual mud-fight. The low spot between the Seminary apartment buildings, that were dubbed "The Fertile Crescent," because the married seminarians had so many children, would fill with water. With a little stirring it was ready with the slimiest mud. The guys would grab the screaming girls and dump them in the mud. They would check first to be sure the girl wasn't wearing some-thing that couldn't stand the mud. Again, if somebody gave a signal, we didn't hear it. Then it became a joke. One of our white friends from the dorm, Liz, decided that even though she was wearing old jeans, she didn't want her hair messed. She asked me and Gwen to walk with her, since she knew we would create an invisible shield around her. We walked past the guys and Liz stuck her tongue out at them. They seemed annoyed, but not the least bit embarrassed that she had noticed the way they excluded us.

We didn't think we had come to Drew to educate these

people, but that's just what we had to do. Gwen internalized it all. When she was struggling with racists in Birmingham, she knew who the enemy was, and at the end of the day she could go home where she knew she had support. At the end of the day at Drew, there were more of those same people asking the same ignorant questions.

I, on the other hand, had Billy. None of us did any real dating that year; we hung out together in groups. I had my boyfriend "Johnnysmith" back home and Gwen had hers. We wrote letters, and telephoned. In the meantime there was Billy. He was from Yonkers, New York and was a music major. We had a couple of classes together, because I told him during orientation week what I planned to take, and he signed up for classes to be near me. Other times he would hang out in the Student Union, playing the piano. He could play all the popular music by ear. His stand-out piece was Ray Charles' "What'd I Say." That would always draw a crowd, and start people making requests for him to play other songs.

Billy asked me to Fall Weekend, November 22-23, 1963. There would be a formal dance on Friday night off-campus and a semi-formal dance on Saturday. My last class on Friday was over at 11. I was alone in my dorm room doing my hair and listening to WABC radio when I heard the report from Dallas that the President had been shot. The reaction from everybody up and down the hall was the same. Seven girls immediately flung doors open and ran into the hall, "Did you hear?" And then there was a rush to use the one pay phone on the floor, to call home and ask, as if we were the only ones who knew the President had been shot.

What followed is all a blur, the huddles of crying girls, and repeating the news each time another person arrived back from class, and the sighing and sobbing. We forgot about Fall Weekend until the florist arrived with our corsages that had been ordered weeks before. Of course, he had been paid, and he delivered. The word came that the Friday night dance had been cancelled. We knew we couldn't enjoy it anyway, but we dressed for our dates, the guys in their rented tuxedos, the girls in whatever they felt like pinning a corsage on. And we sat in the lounges around the campus, eyes glued to the television replay of the events of the day. By eight o'clock we were spent, from the emotions, and the replays. When Gwen and I finally got back to our room alone, we had our personal lament. What would happen to us now? Finally a President who cared enough about black people to put an end to our oppression, and they shot him dead. We cried ourselves to sleep.

Billy and I didn't get to have a real date after that until he decided to show me New York. He planned a Saturday in the City in December, and I was as excited about it as he was. Just getting there was an adventure for me. We walked from the campus to the Erie-Lackawanna train station and took the commuter train to Hoboken. Then we took the PATH tubes into the City, to the Port Authority Bus Terminal.

The City was all decorated for Christmas, and we walked and walked, looking at the store windows and all the lights. I had never had roasted chestnuts, and he bought me some, and New York pretzels and hot dogs. It was better than the county fair. I was delighted with Billy in New York. I just couldn't tell him it was the city that I loved, not him. We went to Radio City Music Hall to see the Christmas Show. The Rockettes were spectacular, but I was just as much taken in by the building, the art-deco, and the bathrooms. That must have been the first time that I learned to check out the bathrooms as a way to measure the experience. The marble and tile and mirrors and the lights everywhere. The movie was Mondo Cane. I was probably watching the theater more than the movie, and taking in the theater, and the music. By the time the movie ended, we could both sing the theme, and we sang it walking out of the theater and all the way home. "More than the greatest love the world has known, this is the love I give to you alone." It became "Our Song," and of course by the next day, Billy was playing it on the piano in the Student Union.

A week later I went home for Christmas, and came back

wearing a ring from Johnnysmith. I had to break Billy's heart, but New York City was in my heart forever.

What if Ralph hadn't Died?

You asked, "What if Ralph hadn't died?" There we go with the "What-ifs" again. The easy answer is, Joshua might not have moved to New York, and I wouldn't have found you. I know your real question is, how would you fit in my life, and would we be having this conversation?

This is the hardest part to put to paper, because of the thoughts I have suppressed and I didn't even allow myself to think through to completion. I told myself I had to protect Ralph's image, or at least Joshua and Mark's image of him. They knew life was not easy with him, that the way he treated me wasn't consistent with the things he said he felt.

The truth is this. He never forgave me for having you. He never forgave me for breaking up with him to be with Jimmy.

I met Ralph at Drew. There were so few blacks on the campus that we considered each other family, and it didn't require introductions. He arrived my sophomore year, as a first year Seminary student. I worked in the dining hall, the early breakfast shift. I have always been a morning person; I would put in a couple of hours in the dining hall, then have classes from eight to noon, and be free the rest of the day. My job was making toast and coffee. I would get the coffee going when I arrived, and then melt a yellow glob of stuff to slather on the toast as it came dropping off the toast machine. I would make a big tray, hundreds of pieces of pre-buttered toast.

Ralph would come through the line around seven every day and ask for toast "with no butter!" and a hard-boiled egg. It got so I would make sure some toast was coming off the machine that I wouldn't slather, and have it ready for him. I didn't do the eggs, but since I knew most were soft-boiled, I reasoned that if I saved one from the early batch that had been sitting on the steam table for long enough, it stood a good chance of being hard boiled by the time he got there.

Seminarians came to Drew at various stages of life, and ranged in age from early 20's to 70's. Ralph was balding, and always wore a vest, so I assumed he was in his late thirties. Boy, was I wrong. He was only twenty-five, but I regarded him as an older gentleman, and there was no attraction there.

My roommate Gwen and I had developed our own way of dealing with the racial discrimination in the dining hall by going on the defense. We discovered during freshman year that if we sat down at a table with white students, they would usually get up and leave. After months of hurt and recrimination, and Gwen spending weeks in the hospital with an ulcer, we found a way to get our own sense of power. We chose the best seats in the place, and if the whiteys wanted to move, then we had the best table to ourselves. So it was, that the long table by the window became the place where the Negro students and our white friends, would sit. The seminarians, black, white, young and old, soon became part of our crowd.

Dinnertimes that had once been the most painful time of day became the most joyous. The discussions were lively and thought-provoking, since the seminarians had no fear of talking about religion and politics. Sometimes they would dominate the discussion with the latest issues from their classes, and Gwen and I, as preacher's kids, would dip into the conversation with our own understanding of the subject. Ralph always had a lot to say, and even the white guys would treat him as an authority figure. I learned that Ralph was a graduate of Morehouse College, a divorcee, and I thought the picture he carried in his wallet of a little girl was his. He was an AME, the son of an AME Presiding Elder. Since I didn't know any AME's (there was an AME Zion church in Petersburg, but no AME Church), I didn't know what Presiding Elder meant, but apparently it was important. Gwen, who was CME, explained it to me later.

I didn't remember that Daddy's "home church" in Forsythe, GA was an AME church. The time we visited one summer when Mother was still alive, they had introduced him as their son returned home. After Daddy spoke for a short time from the pulpit, the minister started the congregation to singing, "Give Me That Old Time Religion." The verses were simple. "It was good for my dear Mother and it's good enough for me." Then it was good for my dear father, brother, Paul and Silas, the Hebrew children, and so on through the Bible. We must have sung a hundred verses before it got so hot in that old wooden frame building that I asked to go out to get a drink from the well. When I asked Daddy later why they sang so many verses, he said the minister was trying to embarrass him. It took me years to understand that some people don't think of Episcopalians as having real religion.

Drew had one black faculty member, a seminary Professor, who happened to be a graduate of Morehouse. Because of that connection, Morehouse College sent a student every semester to participate in Drew's United Nations semester. Students, usually political science majors, would come to Drew from all over the country. They would have two days a week at the UN, for lectures, and three days back at Drew. Once Gwen and I knew to expect a new black man on campus every semester, we would scout out the UN students until we spotted him. We had developed some good friendships with the ones who came our freshman year. Once we learned that Ralph was a Morehouse graduate, we thought we had another connection to the student who came from Morehouse for the semester.

What if Ralph hadn't died?

That was the year we took over the stereo room in the Student Center. Gwen and I had gotten tired of the music played at the official social gatherings, and decided to take our records to the small room with the stereo. Our friends would join us and we would dance to The Impressions, The Temptations, James Brown, and whatever records we had in our personal collections. Sometimes when we got to the room, a few white people would be there, often a couple making out, but when they were outnumbered by blacks, they would leave. So it became "Our Room." Friday or Saturday night, sometimes both, was our time to party. Food wasn't allowed, but we might bring in cups of whatever beverage they had in the dining hall.

That semester, the Morehouse student was Lawrence Perry, and he developed a crush on me. He came to the parties in the Stereo Room, and would dance with the rest of us. Mostly when we danced, everybody was on the floor dancing with everybody else. There weren't any couples. Even so, Lawrence would single me out, especially for the "jerk" and the slow numbers.

One week the dinner table was buzzing about David Lilton's party. David was one of the white seminary students who came from Staten Island, and he had invited all his seminary friends to a party at his house on Friday. Eventually the word went around that Gwen and I could come, as well as Lawrence. When Friday came, Dave had coordinated everybody to meet in the main parking lot, and the few seminarians who had cars piled everybody in, and we went to Staten Island.

The party was held all over the house. We danced and ate, and Dave had some kind of punch. Some people continued the discussion of hermeneutics from class, and some people coupled off. There was one white woman, a seminarian, who followed Ralph around, and every time I saw him, there she was leaning on him. Lawrence followed me around, and every time he cornered me, I said, "Let's dance," and we did. By the time the food and punch were gone, they checked to make sure there were sober people to drive back to campus and we piled into cars again. By this time, there was no getting away from Lawrence, and we wound up squeezed together in the back seat.

That was when he started kissing me. After a couple of kisses, I wasn't interested in any more, so he started nuzzling my neck. What I didn't realize was that he was giving me a gigantic hickey on my neck. When we got back to the dorm we crashed so fast, that nobody noticed the hickey, or maybe it hadn't come to full bloom by then. The next morning, there it was. Gwen laughed until she cried, and ran to get Andi and Binky, and they howled. Meanwhile I was going through every piece of clothing I owned to find a way to cover it. I used a half tube of Cover Girl blemish control on it to try to hide it first, and then wrapped a scarf around my neck. Since it was Saturday, I hid out in the dorm.

By Sunday dinner, I thought I had it under control, even though by then it was quite purple, and quite large. My friends had their laughing under control, and we got through dinner without anybody saying anything. As we were taking our finished trays to the conveyor belt, Ralph said to me, "I'll have to speak to the young brother about how not to leave marks." Ugh!! I was busted. I just put my tray down and tried to get out of the building away from Gwen who was laughing out loud.

After that, Ralph became my advisor when it came to Lawrence. How do I get rid of this guy, and let him down easy? He was a nice guy, but I still had my boyfriend Johnnysmith back home. Ralph was going to take him under his wing as a Morehouse brother.

*   *   *

Ralph had a distinct way of expressing himself. At dinner with all of the seminary students, he usually dominated the conversation, talking loudly, precisely, and slowly. The other seminarians deferred to him, maybe because he was a few years older, maybe because he always wore a vested suit. Whatever it was, they let him say his piece. They might disagree with him after he finished, but they never interrupted. At first he was simply an older friend, and I respected his opinion. When it came to Lawrence Perry, I didn't expect Ralph would take the opportunity to push him out of the picture altogether.

I got used to the way he expressed himself, always with enough ambiguity that you could never tie him down. He never answered a Yes/No question with Yes or No. He would give a response, but not answering the question you asked. If you said, "Isn't it a nice day?" He might respond, "The sky is blue."

I often tell the story of what happened years later at one of our favorite places to eat. We liked Perkins Restaurant, because of the good location, open twenty-four hours, and we could get a good late-night snack. He had gotten into the habit of ordering an omelet. Perkins makes good omelets, four eggs, lots of cheese. Well, I got concerned about all those eggs, and cheese and he noticed the sixty-plus menu on the back of the menu. The sixty-plus omelets used only two eggs, which was plenty for a late-night snack. Ralph passed away when he was fifty-eight, so he didn't reach the age of sixty, but he thought since he was bald he could pass for sixty. He ordered the sixty-plus omelet, and nobody questioned his age. He did this for many months until a new waitress came along. She asked, "Are you sixty?" I knew he wouldn't lie, but I also knew he would weasel out of the question. He answered, "I was born in 1938!!" The waitress couldn't do the math, so she brought him the omelet!!!

The kids and I got in the habit of trying to get a real answer out of him, but we got used to the ambiguous barrier between us and whatever might be the truth in his heart. He would never discuss matters of the heart, our relationship, or our sex life. He was Victorian in many ways, and would be embarrassed if he ever let down his guard.

In spite of it all, we were a team. Maybe he never knew what was in my heart, but, all those years, it worked for us together. Maybe like pieces of a puzzle, the same caramel colored skin, and people said we looked like brother and sister. Even Daddy was pleased when he would have a son in the ministry. When Daddy retired, and all those people came that he had known for years in various parishes throughout Virginia, and they met Ralph, they said he was another Father Gordon.

*   *   *

He never forgave me for Jimmy. I broke up with Ralph to be with Jimmy. It's not like we were married or even engaged. I was nineteen and Ralph was so much older, so serious, so stable. He had said he loved me, and he would be there when I returned from my junior year in Germany. If I had not planned to go to Germany; if I had not needed to complete my other language requirement; if Drew had had a summer session; if I hadn't chosen to go to Howard University that summer, I would never have met Jimmy. And maybe we were placed in the same place at the same time, for the sole purpose of bringing you into the world.

Lynne and I were roommates at Howard for the summer. I had applied to take two semesters of Spanish (simultaneously). They had accepted my application, but then when I registered, they said I couldn't do both together, since the first semester was prerequisite to the second. In practice it wasn't, and I knew that the second semester was focused more on literature, while the first was on grammar, but they wouldn't hear my argument. So I was stuck there for only a three hour Spanish course for the eight-week session.

I remembered why I hadn't applied to go to Howard from high school. So many of my classmates at Coolidge High had gone to Howard that I had developed a prejudice against Howard. Howard was one of the schools that always had a light-skinned girl as homecoming queen in the annual edition of Ebony Magazine that had all the latest Queens from black colleges. I knew from association with the girls at Coolidge that Howard had a tight social caste system that vetted freshmen according to complexion, social status, and clothes. I had friends and family of different complexions, and social status, and I treated them all the same. And I never had enough of the "right" clothes. I had decided I didn't want that kind of distraction for my college years, and chose instead to apply to three white colleges.

That summer at Howard, I decided for the first time in my life, I wasn't the teacher's pet, or the nerd or one of those Negro girls; I would be dateable. My Spanish course would not require much of my time, and since I was there for the whole session, I might as well have fun. For a change, there were many attractive black men around, and I had a social life. I didn't need to fit in with the other girls in the dorm, since I had Lynne as a roommate. There wouldn't be enough time for me there to attempt to adapt to their way of doing things. I felt free, no longer burdened down by the racial situation at Drew, and unencumbered by the social order at Howard. Lynne and her boyfriend, Dick took me with them to weekend parties, and he even tried to fix me up with one of his friends. Nobody in particular appealed to me; I was just having fun.

The Saturday we met Jimmy, Lynne and I had decided to sit on the wall outside of the Quad, to see who we could see. Jimmy and his friend Hal walked by and Hal started trying to hit on Lynne. Lynne had a pretty steady relationship with Dick so she wasn't interested, but she was up for a flirt. Jimmy and I just laughed in the background at the two of them. Hal said they had to pick up some things at the Fine Arts building, and then they were going to get some lunch and asked us to join them. When we hesitated, they both pulled out their wallets to show their student ID cards, and Hal said, "We're not bums off the street, and my man here just graduated," as he pointed to Jimmy. Jimmy had a CIA badge, and Hal joked that Jimmy took out the top-secret trash. So the four of us rode around town together for a few hours, until Lynne decided she needed to be back at the dorm. By then Hal saw he wasn't making any progress with Lynne, and he started on me. Jimmy was kind of laid back, amused at his friend's tactics, taking it all in. Hal finally said he wanted to show me a mural he had done at the home of some of their friends. The three of us continued together to the home of Mr. & Mrs. Farrar, where Hal showed me the mural of a beach scene in their family room. I wasn't impressed, and didn't say much about it. Hal sensed I was holding back, and prodded me to tell. Finally to make him stop prodding, I proceeded to tell Hal what was wrong with the mural.

"The rocks are too soft. With all that ocean pounding against them, they should have sharp edges. The water doesn't move." I laid into him. I thought it would shut him up, but he wouldn't quit. He kept talking the whole time we were there, so the Farrars smiled, amused at his attempts to impress me. When their daughter Beverly came out to join us, it was clear she and Jimmy were more than just friends, but it seemed to be an old, very casual relationship.

When the three of us left, Jimmy still driving, I sat in the front, and Hal sat in the back alone, but continued to dominate the conversation, directed at me. Finally, I said, "Do you ever take a breath!!?" Jimmy, laughed out loud, more animated than

What if Ralph hadn't died?

I had seen him all day. Hal finally got it. "Well, I'll just be quiet, then." We rode the rest of the way in near silence, with Jimmy and me sharing a few pleasantries. When they dropped me off at the dorm, I handed Jimmy a note with my phone number, and said, "Call me," and slipped out of the front seat, while Hal got out of the back, his mouth hanging open.

I had never made the first move like that in my life. I don't know what it was that attracted me to Jimmy. Maybe it was the way he moved, like a warm milk-chocolate panther. I didn't have a particular preference for complexion the way a lot of black people do. In elementary school, I liked the boys who were light-skinned like my Daddy. After I got older, it didn't matter how dark or light a guy was, as long as he moved the right way. Besides, I never made the first move.

Jimmy called me the next day, and we were together every day for the rest of the summer. Jimmy worked the second shift; he said it was a classified position at the CIA, so he couldn't tell me what kind of work he did. I didn't believe it for one minute, but after he drove me to the CIA building, showed his ID to the guard and drove into the parking lot, I didn't question him anymore about it. He said it had something to do with anatomical drawings, and he was always studying a Gray's Anatomy textbook.

Our time was the afternoon, after my class, and before he

had to go to work. We hung out on campus, the Fine Arts building, and his favorite spot on the hill overlooking the reservoir. He showed me off to his friends, even his singing group. They talked about recording, but they seemed to be another one of those groups who started in High School singing Doo-Wop on the corner. They could sound like Sam Cooke, or the Temptations. Jimmy had definite opinions about Smokey Robinson, "He sounds like a woman. If they want a woman's voice in the group, they ought to let the girl sing the lead." We liked the Temptations hit that summer, "Since I lost My Baby." It became the song I would sing for the next few years, when I needed a good cry.

By the end of the first week, I knew I had to come clean with Ralph. I called him in Detroit where he was working for the summer, and told him I was interested in someone else. It made him angry, and he wrote me a letter telling me I would regret giving him up.

*　　*　　*

When I had my period, Jimmy confessed he had been afraid we might have had an accident. And he told me he already had a child, or at least she said it was his child. He had dated her a while, but she was seeing other guys too. He said if I got pregnant, he wouldn't doubt that it was his. We never talked about marriage.

What if Ralph hadn't died?

When the summer session ended, I went home to Emporia to prepare to go to Germany. By then I had all my instructions on what clothing to bring, and how to ship my trunk to the cruise ship Rotterdam that would take the whole group to Europe. I shipped my trunk with winter clothes and personal items for my room in the dormitory. I had applied for my passport while I was in Washington, and awaited its arrival. Everyone in the family and everyone in the community were excited for me. When I missed my period, I knew I was pregnant. I waited until Jimmy came to Emporia to visit before I told him. I wanted to do it in person, so I could see his reaction.

"What do you want to do?"

"I have to go to Germany. I can't have this baby." I couldn't even imagine those words coming out of my mouth. That was what I told him, but I also couldn't imagine telling Daddy I was pregnant. The situation with Toni and her baby had been such a strain on him, even though he never complained. I felt like the whole family thought of me as their last great hope to do something extraordinary. Daddy would be crushed. I thought it might even cause him the fatal heart attack. Besides, since Mother's death I had done it all alone. My life was in my own hands, and if I was to get it right, I had to manage it alone.

I couldn't tell if Jimmy was disappointed or relieved, but he had a plan. He could get me some pills that would make me abort.

"Will you still be here for me when I come back from Germany?" We hadn't had enough time together to even know if we had something that could be permanent, but what we had, I didn't want to let go of.

It was a question I had asked him all summer. He never said he loved me; he just reminded me that he had been with me every day since we met. But he said he would be there. He even talked of coming to visit me in Germany. "I always wanted to travel."

By the end of August, he had sent me pills, and nothing happened. I returned to Washington and stayed with George and Shirley so Jimmy could take me to a doctor that had a reputation for giving out pills. I took more pills, and still nothing happened. By then the tension between us had started where there had never been tension before. I couldn't ask him to marry me, and he never broached the subject.

We managed one last visit before I went to New York to board the ship to Europe. By then I was emotional, pregnant, anxious about the trip, nauseous from the pregnancy, unhappy with leaving him, unhappy that he never mentioned marriage, and sure that I would never see him again. I said I would see a doctor in Germany. We said we would write.

Morning Sickness and Seasick

How could I not go? Everybody in Emporia knew Sarah was going to study abroad. My passport had arrived, and I had to get my immunizations. The doctor in Emporia did it all. I was sure he could look at me and tell that I was pregnant, but he didn't say anything. Everyone was caught up in the excitement except for me. I had my itinerary, an eight-day cruise aboard the Rotterdam with all the Junior Year in Munich and Freiburg students and some of the staff to orient us aboard the ship to living in Europe. The program was through Wayne State University and students from other colleges effectively transferred to Wayne State for the year in order to participate. There were three of us from Drew in the Junior Year in Munich (JYM) and two from Drew who would go to the JYF program in Freiburg. We would go by bus from Rotterdam to Freiburg and Munich with stops and tours through Germany. I was numb for what should have been the most exciting experience of my life.

Since I had experience traveling alone to New Jersey and New York, I didn't need anyone to take me to the port of NY for my departure. I arranged to go a couple of days ahead to stop at Drew to say goodbye to my friends that I wouldn't see for a year. At least that's what I told Daddy. What I didn't tell him was that most of my real friends were doing a Junior Year program somewhere else, England, France, Belgium, and they were all in the process of packing and getting to their points of departure. I used the time to go to Washington to say good-bye to Jimmy.

That last time together was awful. He didn't have time for me, and seemed impatient for me to leave. We said our good-bye's and I went on to Drew, where I spent the night in the women's dorm before my departure. Michael came to the port to see me off. In those days visitors could come aboard into the cabins for Bon Voyage parties. I was in a big cabin with four other girls in the JYM program. They were girls from Wellesley, Bryn Mawr, and Sarah Lawrence. I was feeling way out of my league. It helped that Michael was there, since he would talk to anybody and everybody. The parents of the Bryn Mawr girl brought in bottles of Champagne to toast our journey.

I managed to detach from my pregnancy and focus on all the things that were happening on this trip. There were days when I was nauseous, and I didn't know if it was seasickness or the pregnancy. Since other people were throwing up, nobody paid much attention to me.

Everything was a new experience for me. Some of the others had been on cruises before, and knew that food was abundant and could be brought to the cabin if we wanted. They went to the midnight buffets, while I preferred to go to bed at a sensible time; the pregnancy made me too tired to stay up anyway. During the day we had orientation: How to hold our knife and fork like a European, how to order in a restaurant, how to sit with strangers since Europeans expect to share their table when space is limited, how to tip, how talk on the telephone (don't answer "Hello"), how to count. You would think we knew our numbers in German from day one in high school German, but we had to learn the Bavarian way, and the dialectical numbers, like "zwo." Even counting on our fingers was different. We count forefinger as "one" through the pinky as "four" and the thumb is "five." Germans start with the thumb as "one," so if we wanted to buy two of something by pointing with two fingers, the seller would assume we had started with the thumb and would give us three. Counting money, understanding the nicknames for coins, telling time, and behavior in the lecture hall in the university were all different from what I might expect. The students rap on the desk to applaud the entrance of the professor, and it was not unusual to boo and hiss a professor if you didn't like what he had to say. They taught us where to shop, and how to buy student tickets for cultural events. We felt like aliens being briefed for a landing.

Since it had been three months since I had spoken any German, and I had taken Spanish during the summer, this was a good time to get back in practice speaking German. We spoke German all day in our orientation classes, and some of the students wanted to speak German at meals and in our cabins. My table in the dining room was more of a party crowd, and all they wanted to talk about was where they would go on the weekends and what was a good place to go skiing. I sank into invisible mode, and nobody cared.

When we arrived in Rotterdam, where we would spend the first night, we got the first shock. Dutch people didn't want to hear us speak German to them. They wanted it to be clear that they had no part in the atrocities of World War II. We could understand them since the languages are similar, and they could understand us in German, but they insisted, in English, "We are not German!!" So we had to put off our use of German until we crossed the border in a couple of days.

We spent hours on the bus going from museums, to churches, to birth places of artists, to castles and government buildings and various points of interest. There were often places where we had to climb up into clock towers to get the best view of the city. Many times I had to sit down on the stairs when I became dizzy and nauseous. At every stop I was the first to ask for a toilet, and I had to remember not to ask for a bathroom, since I wouldn't be taking a bath. We became experts in the architecture of ancient churches and opera houses whether

Renaissance, Baroque, Rococo, Neo-classical or Modern as well as the paintings and sculpture of the periods. It should have earned us additional credit in art appreciation for all the knowledge we were getting. On the bus we sang. We were given pages of lyrics to all the well-known German folk and hiking songs, drinking songs, and national songs. We were totally immersed in all that being German might mean. When we stopped at Oberammergau, the town that produces a Passion Play every ten years, we could sing as a "round," *"Ob er aber über Oberammergau, Oder aber über Unterammergau. Oder ob er überhaupt nicht kommt, ist nicht g'wiß!"* A couple of students brought their guitars from home, and we mixed the latest folk and anti-war songs from the States with the German songs. One of the favorites was Pete Seeger's "Where Have all the Flowers Gone?"

When we finally arrived in Munich, we felt ready, but next came the process of admission into the university, getting settled into our various housing options, and applying for student visas. Those of us from Drew had been told by upper-classmen who had been in the JYM program, that we should choose to live in the dorm. The housing form had given us a choice of the dorm or living "with a family." The "family" option most of the time turned out to be a room in a rooming house, with no contact with a German family at all. Only a rare few found themselves with a family whom they could see and talk to on a daily basis. The ones from our group, who found themselves in a rooming house, had no cooking privileges, and limited bath access.

I checked into the Max Kade Haus in Studentenstadt Freimann where I would have a roommate in a room twice the size of the dormitory rooms at Drew. We had Danish Modern furniture, ample closet space, a sink in the room, and a kitchen and bathroom down the hall. I paid less than $20 per month plus $2 for laundry -- towel and sheets changed weekly. My classmates in the rooming house quickly learned how to come and visit so they could get a shower every now and then. My roommate didn't arrive until the start of the semester in October. I knew by then that the first semester would end in February and we would have two months' break before returning in May for the summer semester. I had calculated that my due date would be in April so I was already planning how I could give birth during the break and not miss any time in class.

Once I finally had a mail address, I wrote to Jimmy several times per week. I had no idea how long a letter would take to arrive in the States or how long it would take for a return letter, if he wrote. The more I wrote, the more anxious I became that I didn't hear from him. I had bought some little souvenirs during the trip from Rotterdam, and sent them to him. I finally heard from him after I sent a Zwetschchen Mensch I bought at a craft fair in Nürnberg. It was a little doll made from prunes that was customarily used for good luck, much like a kitchen witch. I imagine when he received it, it looked like some kind of voodoo doll. It did get his attention and he wrote me asking what in the world it was. I continued to write lots of newsy letters, and received only a few responses back from him.

The only other black person in the JYM program was Elaine, who amazingly was from a town not fifty miles from Daddy's church in Emporia. She was a student from Bennett College, the kind of girl who would have been classified as a "brain' and would have been excluded from social activities with her own consent. We might have been friends, but she seemed to resent my being there -- another black woman to invade her turf and her position as the only German-speaking black. Since I was pregnant and avoiding social connections, that was fine with me. I feared that if I got too close, the word of my condition could travel back to Daddy.

Elaine would have been a pretty girl if she didn't have such an attitude. You know how when we get excluded so much we carry ourselves as if to say, "I didn't want to be friends with you anyway." She had long black hair, smooth brown complexion. You wouldn't even have noticed the corrective shoes if she hadn't foisted them in your face so prominently. She was a girl who didn't know her own beauty. As it turned out, she lived in

117

the Max Kade Haus as well, on another floor, but we rarely saw each other in the building.

The Junior Year in Munich program operated out of large apartment on Akademiestraße near the University. Fräulein Doktor Marianne Brockhoff was the director of the program, and her office was there. There was a large space that was big enough for the twenty of us to meet with the tutors who would manage our curriculum and grading. We would attend lectures at the University, but in order to have a grade that could be transferred back to our home colleges, we would meet with the tutors weekly for discussions and assignments. We also had tutors for grammar and colloquial language who gave us weekly writing assignments. They helped us with course selection and the registration process for the University courses that started in October. We had plenty to do to be ready for that first time in the University.

Doktor Brockhoff had her personal apartment upstairs in the same building. She was probably in her forties, but since the staff called her Fräulein Doktor, that meant they considered her still marriageable. Older women were usually called Frau even if they were not married. She reminded me of some of the actresses I knew from foreign films, like Marlene Dietrich or Ingrid Bergman. She wasn't nearly as physically striking as the stars, but she had that same regal nature of a woman of substance who had a past. While the men on the staff were formal and stilted, Fräulein Doktor was more friendly and nurturing. She had cared for the groups of American students like a mother hen for many years.

I registered for three lectures at the University: Germanistik, Philosophie, and the Romantik Period. At the JYM office I would have the language course with Herr Schmidt, and a course on German Drama. The Drama course had assignments that coincided with plays that would be performed in Munich, and we were assigned to attend them.

The JYM office was where we gathered during the day, between lectures at the Uni, and for general socializing. There was always a game of bridge going on, and people would bring their snacks to eat or share. There were three bakeries between the JYM office and the Uni, and all of us sampled the different pastries -- the strudel, the tortes, and the kuchen. And there were fruit stands outside when fruit was in season. There was always plenty of food. The apartment also had a large bathroom, so the students living in rooming houses could take a real bath there as well.

As students at the University, we could get a tram pass for fifteen Marks each month so that we could ride all the trams and buses throughout the city any time we wanted. I got into a routine riding the tram from my dormitory into the heart of the city, where I would buy yogurt and fruit for breakfast, or sometimes stop for a boiled egg and toast. My budget was going to be easy. While some of my wealthy classmates studied the latest "Europe on Five Dollars a Day" for the inexpensive places to visit, I was managing quite well on two dollars a day. I shopped at the butcher occasionally and took something home to cook in the dormitory kitchen down the hall.

By the time my roommate arrived I thought I was well settled in, but she still had to show me more of the ropes. First I hadn't made my bed correctly. The bed was a Swedish style day-bed with a heavy foam mattress that was about four inches thick, and very comfortable. The laundry that cost two dollars per month provided towels and "sheets" -- one big thing that I decided was to cover the mattress like a pillow, and a flat sheet I used to cover myself. I didn't know what I would do for a blanket when the weather got cold. My roommate, Ina explained that the thing I was using like a pillowcase for my mattress was in fact a case for my Federbett, stored in the bin under the window. Aha!! That was so much easier to do. And the flat sheet covered the mattress. Then she showed me where we each had space to store dry goods in the kitchen, as well as a basket in the refrigerator for each person. There was also a Canteen in the main building of the dormitory where I could buy pastries and yogurt much cheaper than at the bakeries.

Morning Sickness and Seasick

I was eating well, trying not to gain too much weight, and also trying to save a little money each month to cover whatever unknown expenses I would have. It should have been the most exciting time of my life, but I was pregnant and alone in a foreign country, *a long way from home*. I cried myself to sleep every night for months.

Christmas in Munich

After I had gotten past the first trimester of my pregnancy, I didn't have morning sickness anymore, and I was able to concentrate more on my school work. Herr Schmidt insisted we all needed to get out and meet people in order to improve our command of the German language. I wasn't up for meeting people, but I did go to concerts and plays. Every month after my $100 was transferred to the bank in Munich, I would pay my room rent, and laundry bill, and have plenty left over to buy tickets. Many of my classmates would wait until the night of a production and get student tickets from those that were unsold. I did it a few times. I saw my first opera in the Bayerische Opernhaus from a fifth row seat in the orchestra. Lohengrin was a fantastically beautiful production in that gorgeous building. Most of the time, though, I bought tickets at the beginning of the month, so I would feel obligated to go out when the date came. I didn't have any problem with going alone, and sometimes I might strike up a conversation with someone sitting beside me, or at intermission. I was a bit of a curiosity, since most Germans didn't know what I was.

My roommate Irmgaard was friendly enough. She had had

a roommate the previous year from the Junior Year program, so she was used to training Americans. The previous roommate's name was Susan, and all I heard the first few weeks, was "Susan did it this way," and "Susan and I took turns with that." Susan was of German descent and her German was obviously better than mine from the beginning. Besides, even though "Ina" as she liked to be called, didn't make an issue of my being black, I still thought of her as a white girl. We had long conversations about life in the US, me with my German dictionary in my lap to look up words I didn't know, and she gradually came to understand that I wasn't Susan.

We had a continuing argument about whether America has any culture of its own. Ina insisted that since all of the music, art, and creative expression originated somewhere else that America has no culture. I reminded her of the music that comes from the slave experience of black people. While it has its roots in Africa, most of the development of jazz, and rhythm and blues is purely American. After many nights of disagreeing, I played my Dinah Washington "Unforgettable" album for her. She was taken in by Dinah's sultry voice, and conceded. I didn't tell her until weeks later that it was my "crying record," the one that helped me release any pent-up pain and just cry.

Ina would talk about her parents who were divorced. She didn't get along with her father, had lost contact with him, and her mother lived near Bonn. Her father thought life was better under Hitler, and he hated the new government. He named her Irmgaard, a real Aryan name. That's why she preferred to be called Ina, the name her mother called her. Her grandmother still lived in the East Zone; she hadn't tried to get out before the Wall went up, and only later understood how life changed for her. Her biggest complaint was not being able to get fresh fruits and vegetables. Ina was already planning to find some green bananas to send to her so they would be ripe in time for Christmas.

After weeks of having Ina prod me to get out more, I finally told her I was pregnant. It was good to get it out, so I wouldn't have to continue to hide while in the room. She hadn't noticed my expanding belly. We talked long into the night about how it happened, and what I was going to do. I still didn't know. I didn't tell her I had considered giving my baby up for adoption in Germany. I had given up that idea after encountering many *Besitzungskinder*, children fathered by black GI's, who seemed like lost souls in Aryan-land. Ina started prodding me to tell someone at home. I wasn't ready for that yet, but I did write to Gwen, Andi, Binky and Neil. Gwen and Andi were in London for the London Semester in political science. Binky was at Drew preparing for the second semester in Aix-en-Provence. Neil was doing a post-graduate study in London.

I heard back from everybody rather quickly except for Neil. We had stayed in touch since he had spent a semester at Drew for the UN Semester, and I still considered him a good friend. Gwen and Andi wrote that they would come to spend Christmas with me. Their semester ended in December, and they had planned to travel some before going home. My plight gave them a good excuse to come to Germany. Binky wrote a very supportive letter, and told me of her current relationship issues.

That lightened my heart to know they would be coming. The University would be closed for two weeks for Christmas, and Ina along with most of the other German students would be going home for Christmas. When I told Ina my friends were coming, she readily said that one could sleep in her bed, and she enlisted our friend Birgit from next door to volunteer her bed as well. I was looking forward to a German Christmas. I was expecting snow, and decorations, and singing all the German Christmas Carols I knew.

I needed Ina to help me find a Doctor for prenatal care. "Obstetrician" was not a word I could find in my English/German dictionary, and my wandering the streets in neighborhoods where I saw Doctors' offices had not helped me decipher that specialty either. She laughed at the way I had been searching, and told me I needed a Doktor who was a Geburtshelfer or a Doktor of Gynäkologie. She gave me the name and address of the doctor she went to for "Anti-Baby Pillen."

When I wrote to Jimmy to tell him I had seen a Doctor, he responded in about 10 days that I should be careful that I didn't see a quack and that he didn't want me to suffer any harm. He was still thinking of abortion, when I had gotten way past that. I could feel the life in me, and it wasn't just a missed period anymore.

Munich was in the midst of Fasching, which is the German equivalent of Mardi Gras, except it starts on November 11 (11/11) at 11:11 AM and continues until the beginning of Lent. The big parties start leading up to Christmas. Ina and her boyfriend Peter were going out every weekend to a Fasching party, and they invited me to come. I declined and enjoyed the quiet back in the dorm, except for the sounds of fireworks.

I bought Christmas presents as I always did for my friends, and I usually spent under ten dollars for some trinket that was more for the thought than the value of it. I considered Ina a friend, and I bought her a leather cigarette case for thirty-five Marks, about eight dollars. When I gave her the gift before she left for the holiday, she explained to me that Germans usually give some kind of food treat or craft item for Christmas, making me feel I had been too extravagant with my eight dollars. She in turn gave me a package of Lebkuchen, an iced gingerbread cookie she knew that I liked, and is traditional for German

Christmas in Munich

Christmas.

Neil was the first of my friends to arrive, even though he had not answered my letter. He knew how to find his way around the city, since he had spent a semester in Germany himself, and he just showed up at the dorm. He didn't expect me to look so…soo..pregnant. I could see he was hurt. We talked for about thirty minutes, and then he made some excuse about having to meet someone, said he would call me, and he was gone.

The next day, I met my friends Gwen and Andi at the train station when they arrived, and we rode the tram back to the dormitory. We hugged all around in the train station. Later they inspected my pregnant self and said I looked cute. I told them about Neil's reaction, and they shook their heads. Gwen said, "You know he always cared about you." We spent hours and hours laughing and talking in the dorm. Andi and Gwen dragged Birgit's bed into my room so we could be together in the same room. We went out and around Munich for a couple of days, and ate dinner out.

One night when we were having dinner in a German restaurant, a group of American GI's was sitting at a table next to us and struck up a conversation. The post-war presence in Germany was still quite great. Germans were used to seeing black men in the cities, but black women were rare. The black GI's were happy to see me and Gwen, and said they hadn't seen a

"Sapphire" in months. We laughed at being called "Sapphire" since it was an obvious reference to the wife of Kingfish in Amos 'n Andy. If it weren't so funny, we would have been insulted, since Sapphire was a nagging wife whose most prominent feature was her butt. We pulled our tables together and planned to meet again on Christmas Day. After they talked about how homesick they were, especially for Christmas, we invited them to have Christmas dinner with us in the dorm.

I had asked Daddy to send me food for Christmas, a Virginia ham and some canned collard greens. I knew the cured ham would keep even without refrigeration. Since there wasn't enough space in my basket in the refrigerator down the hall, I kept it in the shipping box under my bed. My friends and I prepared a mini-feast for Christmas, with that ham, and the greens. Gwen made Macaroni & cheese and biscuits. Andi made some green beans and I baked a pound cake spiked with rum. Three of the GI's came for dinner, and we had a good meal. Afterwards we went up on the roof to watch the Fasching fireworks. It was the first time since I had been in Germany that I felt happy.

My friends had their return tickets to fly back to the US from London, and their rail passes to get back from Munich. We said our tearful goodbyes in the train station, and I thanked them for spending Christmas with me.

The Nazi Factor

When I came back to New York in 1966 it was to give birth. Jimmy knew I was coming, but he was not responding to my letters. Ralph knew I was coming. I must have written everybody who ever said they loved me. Gwen and Andrea were back in the States. Gwen was doing the Washington Semester, but Andrea was back at Drew, and had talked to Ralph.

This time I saw another side of New York. The first two weeks, I lived with my brother Michael in his studio apartment. I slept on his convertible sofa, and he slept in his recliner. All the while he was trying to find a place where I could stay and have my medical needs taken care of. Through his connections in the Episcopal Church he was able to get me into Dana House, a Home for Unwed Mothers. Some women can get into incubator mode, so everything feeds that growing child, and the rest of the world can go away. That was the only way I managed to get through those months in Munich. By the time I got to Dana House, it was such a relief to be away from the prying eyes of the other Junior Year in Munich students, and the Nazis who were our tutors while we attended classes at the Uni. Of course, they weren't all Nazis. The Director, Fräulein Doktor Brockhoff, had helped me make arrangements to get to New York, allowed me to take my semester exams two weeks early, and had assured me that I could come back for the second semester. Even she said that her secretary was a meddling old maid. I was into my eighth month of pregnancy by the time one of the tutors, Herr Schmidt seemed intent upon exposing me in class. It was almost funny how he wrote words on the board to make sure we knew how to spell them, then managed to use the German word for pithy, pregnant in the figurative sense, *prägnant*, as much as he could. Then he wrote it on the board in big block letters with a big exclamation point. What did he expect, that I would jump up crying and say, "Yes, you're right, I'm pregnant!!!" and throw myself on his mercy? Old NAZI!! By the time the Nazi bunch had gone to report me to Fräulein Doktor, I had already decided that I needed to go back to the States. The idea of having a baby in Germany, Plan B, was out, and I had written to my brother Michael, and he had responded that I could come to New York.

Years later, my other siblings probably wondered why I had gone to Michael and not to one of them. It had been a very simple choice for me, since Michael was the only one still single. We had always been close, and became even closer when I started to college at Drew in New Jersey, while he was living in New York. He invited me to New York several times for the weekend. What he didn't know was that I used his name many times more to sign out of the dorm for the weekend to go elsewhere. I had ridden with him on holidays to visit Bobby when Bobby was in the Army, stationed in Schenectady, NY, and when we went home to Virginia for holidays. The summer following my freshman year, we were both there in Emporia with Daddy and our stepmother, Sophie, for most of the summer. And I knew this about Michael -- he was never judgmental, and was always honest with me.

I didn't expect to like living at Dana House, but it quickly gave me a sense of comfort. The girls ranged in age from twelve to 20-something. We came from all kinds of circumstances, with the only common thing being unmarried and pregnant. It was a big old eight-story brownstone on East 72nd Street that had once been the home for a wealthy New York family. There were several large sitting rooms, a chef's kitchen, large dining room, and three floors with two large bedrooms on each floor. I shared a room with three other girls. One girl couldn't stand any light in the room when she slept at night, and we had to close the blinds and pull the heavy shades until the room was so dark you could hardly see your hand in front of your face. I was fortunate to have the bed close to the door, so I could see at least a little sliver of light under the door, just enough that I wouldn't have nightmares of being shut up in a tomb.

I was there the day the twelve-year-old arrived. All the girls buzzed about how young she was. I remembered that I still played with dolls when I was her age. Then I remembered how Benny Anderson had drowned the year after Mother died. Some people said it was a suicide. Benny was fifteen and his girlfriend Lisa was only thirteen when her parents found out she was pregnant. Lisa's Dad tracked Benny down one day when he was walking home from school and beat him up. When they sent Lisa away somewhere, the story was that she went away to school. They found Benny in the river. All the girls at school cried half the day when we heard it. Some of my friends went to view the body at the funeral home, and said he was so swollen that they didn't recognize him. The rumor was that he had left his clothes in a pile, and had drawn a heart with his and Lisa's initials in the dirt before he went into the river. There wasn't any way for a pregnant teenager to keep a baby in those days. I had heard of some promiscuous girls getting illegal abortions, but "nice" girls had to go away. By the time I had graduated from high school in Washington, I knew of several girls who had gone to back-alley abortionists, and had died from infection or had bled to death.

We walked everywhere from Dana House, often in groups

of four or more. The neighbors would giggle when we waddled past, but we had the comfort of each other, so it didn't bother us. We went to all the museums within walking distance, and often visited the Guggenheim and the Museum of Modern Art. "Walking distance" grew longer if we had company, and we walked from the east 70's all the way to Macy's at Herald Square. And of course, we took a buddy or three when we went for checkups at New York Hospital.

I think the hospital was the worst part of it. All of us had our healthcare bill covered by Medicaid, and even though this was no ghetto clinic, we were treated like something the cat dragged in. It was a teaching hospital, so it was not uncommon to have a class of medical interns walk in to watch examinations. I had never had an internal gynecological exam. I had been to an OB/GYN in Munich for regular visits, but he examined me with my clothes on, and checked my urine, what there was of it. He had put me on restricted fluids, only one quart a day, to reduce swelling of my feet, and stop the nausea. I was just happy that he had not prescribed thalidomide. It had already been withdrawn from the market, but a few of the women I saw in the waiting room of my doctor in Munich brought their severely deformed babies with them.

The other girls had told me the internal exam would hurt. I couldn't imagine why, but when my turn came, a kindly nurse held my hand while the intern warmed the metal clamp in running water, inserted it, and then opened it so that it pinched my flesh. I told him he was hurting me. He made a comment under his breath about what I should have told my boyfriend. I was too embarrassed at being there to stand up for myself. I just wanted the exam to be over. It wasn't until my fourth visit that I had a real doctor who put the speculum in right, so I hardly felt a thing.

We had our regular exams, healthy meals at Dana House, and visits with a counselor from Social Services to help us plan what to do with the baby. One of my roommates had taken off time from work to have her baby, and intended to raise it alone. Her family had objected and had sent her to Dana House to make sure she had proper medical attention, and with the hope that she would change her mind about what to do with the baby. We knew each other only by first name, and we were discouraged from communicating again after we left Dana House. They wanted us to be able to get on with our lives, and not look back.

It was March, my baby was due in April, and the Junior Year program would resume in May. I could go back and continue my education without missing much. While my Junior Year classmates were vacationing all over the continent, I was wrestling with the biggest decision of my life. Miss Lipska, my social worker, was very sympathetic, never blaming or accusatory. She tried to make me think I had choices, but she always steered me to the choice of adoption. No, I could never see my baby again. No, I wouldn't know who adopted her. No, I wouldn't know if she was adopted.

I had already decided that it was a girl, and I would name her Teal Heather. I had not picked out a boy's name. I had written to Jimmy asking if he would sign the papers for the baby to have his name, and he had said no. He didn't see any point in it. He wouldn't even sign to acknowledge paternity.

Miss Lipska was strongly against the idea of my traveling immediately back to Munich. I had an open return ticket, and I intended to book my return flight as soon as I gave birth. She said there would be papers to sign, and it would endanger my health and recovery. I knew the baby would go into foster care until she was adopted, and the thought of staying there in New York set me into depression. I was already working on my Plan C, to find myself a husband so I could claim my baby when I returned.

The only time I traveled by subway in New York that year was to visit my social worker. Sometimes she would come to Dana House, but other times when there were papers to review, and other people to see, I would go to her office. I had learned to travel the subways when I was dating Billy. It was just a matter of reading the map and following the signs that led to even more signs. Nobody bothered me in the subway. New York let me be invisible, so I could think.

I asked Jimmy if he would come to see his baby. How could he not come to see his child born? Didn't the pride in the birth of his own child transcend everything, even uncertainty, even whatever rift there was between us? He called twice. It was the same way for any of the girls who received a phone call from the father of her child. She would return to her room with red eyes to her sisters who shared the pain, and stroked her with their eyes, and helped her to allow her heart to break. He called to say he wouldn't come, not even to see her in the hospital. No, he didn't want his name on the birth certificate. It would only be symbolic. If Teal was adopted, then that original birth certificate would be locked away in some adoption bureaucracy forever.

The day I first felt labor pains, it was a week before my due-date. I knew the drill from the other girls who had gone before me. Go to the Dana House nurse, Nurse Adams and she would check and time my contractions. My contractions were 10 minutes apart from the start, so the nurse called a taxi and took me to the hospital. Like many of the girls who were anxious to get on with it, I had a false alarm, the first of two more. I called my brother Michael when I got back to Dana House to keep him informed. When the time came that they did keep me at the hospital, Nurse Adams phoned Michael, but he didn't return the call.

Years later, when my Teal asked me about her birth, I told her that the worst part was being alone. Michael didn't come, and the other girls that I would go for walks with didn't come. I learned later that Michael had gone to Petersburg for Lynne's marriage, and my friends from Dana House were in various stages of labor as well. I had had no training, no preparation for child-birth. Nurse Adams had talked to us about proper breathing, but she didn't train us in Lamaze techniques. My OB nurse treated me with disdain. It was a continuous stream of "What do YOU want?" "What are YOU crying about?" and "You should have thought about that nine months ago." I remember that there was pain, but I don't remember the quality or intensity.

When I looked on that sweet baby face, all I could do was cry. She was a calm and serious baby, and I knew she looked like me. She looked perfectly fine, with the right number of fingers and toes, and tiny baby lashes. When they brought her to me for feeding, I held on tight, savoring every minute that would have to last me a lifetime. The doctor said there were a few seconds that she didn't breathe, and she had a thrush infection. She would have to stay in the hospital after I was discharged, so they could treat the thrush and observe her for any brain damage. Miss Lipska came to take me back to Dana House, and we talked about the next steps. Teal would go into a foster home after the doctors gave the all clear, and I could sign release papers for her to be adopted.

I asked again, "Will you tell me when she is adopted?"

She answered, "No."

"Will I know if she is all right?"

Again, "No." And again she insisted that I needed to stay in New York City. This time, I was the one to say No. I called the airline that day and reserved my seat on the next available flight to Munich. I saw Teal once more before I left. She was in foster care by then, and I still could not sign those papers. I took photographs of her that I kept until the day I could give them to her. I would go back to Germany with Plan C in mind; find a father for my Teal.

When I talked to Doktor Brockhoff, she had given me an absolute date to return since the first week of May, the whole JYM program would take a bus to Berlin and spend a week there. If I didn't make it to Berlin, I would have to drop out of the program. I got back to Munich with only two days to spare. My classmates were surprised to see me, but didn't know what to say other than "Hello." I expected that it would be another semester of invisibility.

By the time we boarded the bus for Berlin, though, the excitement overrode every other concern anybody had over my being there. We would travel through East Germany to Berlin.

Again we had orientation for the trip. We could not take any newspapers or published written material into the east, not in the bus and not in our luggage. Any money we changed into East German Marks would have to be spent or left there. We would have to stop at the border for customs inspection, and must take it seriously since they could detain the whole busload of us if they thought there was any violation of immigration or customs laws. We would not be allowed to stop again until we reached Berlin.

It was another singing and festive bus trip. We knew all the songs from the previous fall, and some students had learned more from visits to the Hofbräu Haus. One of the guitarists had learned the German words to the Pete Seeger song as we heard sung by Marlene Dietrich, *"Sag' mir wo die Blumen sind"* and we sang along with him. When we reached the border, we had to get out of the bus and walk across a disinfecting pad to prevent the spread of Hoof and Mouth disease from West Germany to the east. We did as we were told and kept our questions to ourselves. The armed soldiers opened the luggage compartment and counted the number of pieces, and inspected the passenger compartment of the bus while we were out wiping our shoes. When we reboarded and were on our way we breathed a sigh of relief, and then started the discussion of how ridiculous that inspection had been.

What about the shoes in our luggage? Aren't they infected too? Since we're not going to walk around on East German soil anyway, how could we infect the animals? We all decided it was one of their propaganda moves to impress upon us that their country doesn't have the same disease that the animals in the West have.

We noticed the stark contrast between the east and west right away. Even going through the countryside, we saw that East Germany was locked in time in a world before WWII. Old vehicles, old farm equipment, and thin, pale people who seemed sheltered from the light of day.

Arriving in Berlin we felt like Dorothy arriving in Emerald City. Suddenly the world was in color, and modern. West Berlin was more modern even than Munich. Everything that had been bombed in the war had been replaced and was all new. The streets were wide, and avenues were lined with trees. We were already experiencing the Föhn, the exhilaration that comes from the warm current over the mountains, and the days in May were so long, that it seemed night never came.

We had our schedule of classes already for the week. We would learn about German government and politics, the history since the war, and we would visit certain historic monuments, including that ever-present Wall. West Berlin was a free island inside East Germany, created after World War II. At first the borders of that half of the city were vulnerable, allowing people to come and go, many disappearing from the communist sector and escaping to the west. Then overnight in 1961, the wall sprang up at first like a city wall, then incorporating the walls of buildings. People in some apartment buildings that happened to be on the line between East and West woke up to find that they were living in the Wall. By the time we were there, the people had been removed from those buildings and the windows were bricked in. We could walk along the West side and touch the Wall, the parts topped with barbed wire and broken glass. We spotted a small child playing ball against the wall, who was too young to remember when there was no Wall. There were huge billboards in German on the West side intended for the guards who patrolled the East side. One read, "He who murders, even on command, is accountable." It was a chilling leftover taste of war.

We had time to go to East Berlin on our own and we had instructions for how to conduct ourselves through the immigration process again. The simplest way would be to take the train, and our passports would be checked at each end. The inspector might ask to see our money, and they would prevent us from returning with any eastern currency. Some students decided to walk across the border at Checkpoint Charlie so as to get that historic stamp on their passports. We were advised the immigration inspection there would be more thorough, and the line would move slowly. I went with two other girls by train.

Only one street, Unter den Linden, in East Berlin had been cleaned up after the war. Here it was twenty years later, and there was still evidence of bombing. The city lay mostly in rubble. We visited the Brecht Theater that was patched together, and we walked through parks. We stopped at an outside café on Unter den Linden to have coffee, hoping to be able to talk to someone. An elderly gentleman joined us, but continually looked over his shoulder at the armed soldiers who sat nearby. One of the girls brought cigarettes. She didn't smoke, but somebody had told her it was a good way to get some conversation. She offered our old man a cigarette, and he took it. We talked a while about life in the east. He said it was better under Hitler. At least then they could get fresh vegetables, and didn't have to stand in line for potatoes. He was particularly curious about where I came from and asked if I had freedom in the US. It was clear he had seen news reports of the Civil Rights marches and more recently the riots in Watts that surely played into the Eastern propaganda about the U.S. I told him "It's getting better. We can eat in restaurants now." I was intentionally sarcastic, and he smiled. There was kindness in his eyes, the old Nazi.

On days when we had class, we all had lunch together in a restaurant reserved by the JYM program. Fräulein Doktor had told us this was the season for Berliner Weisse beer. Light beer mit Schluss -- strawberry syrup!! I had not had beer at all during the first semester, and now was my time to learn. It was not unusual to see families with children order a liter or two of beer, and mix a small glass of it with mineral water and give it to young children. There was no age limit for drinking beer.

It was also the season for the Maikäfer, the May bug. There weren't any real ones in the city, but we saw plenty whimsical decorations that included the bug. They reminded me of the June bugs that were so prominent in Petersburg in the summertime.

At night, you would think we didn't have an early schedule in the morning, because after the group dinner, we were off exploring the Berlin night life. There were more modern clubs and discos than were in Munich, with a heavy influence from the US. And since the sun didn't go down in May, but hovered under the horizon, it never got dark. Most of us were hanging out in a large group, so I didn't have to go it alone for a change. One night we went to the Playboy Club, or so it was named even though it had no connection to the Hugh Hefner Empire. We sat at tables for four people; each table featured a telephone, with a four-digit number for the phone printed on the lampshade at the table. We quickly noticed that strangers could call us from around the dance floor on that phone, and it was easy to meet people and laugh and dance. It was great fun for one night. Another night we went to a discothèque that showed music videos on one wall of the place. The big hit that they showed a half dozen times that night was a German version of the old Coasters hit, "Along came Jones," with a campy character that tied the girl up on the railroad track. Another more romantic video was Frank Sinatra's "Strangers in the Night," that was an international hit that year. I came to know more about my classmates during that week than I had the whole previous semester.

When we got back to Munich, I was included more in activities, since I wasn't trying to hide anymore. I even tried my hand at bridge, since the volunteers that were at the Dana House had given me some lessons. I wasn't much good at bridge, but when they got desperate for a fourth during our free times at the JYM office, they would call me over.

Secrets and Intrigue

They say two people can't keep a secret. By the time I went back to Drew, all of my closest confidantes knew the secret, all of the students in the Junior Year program knew, only two of whom went to Munich from Drew, and my brother Michael knew. I was going to hold my head up and go on as if nothing had happened.

I saw that the good thing about Drew was as a black person, I felt invisible anyway. All the people who cared enough to know me were in my confidence. Since there were so many of our class who had studied abroad, whether in England, Belgium, Spain, Germany, France, or Scotland there was plenty buzzing about all the Junior Year abroad stories, and there were enough other secret adventures of people doing drugs, coming out of the closet, nearly getting thrown into prison in the USSR, that my little story of having a baby, was barely a blip on the radar screen.

All the time I had been in New York City living in Dana House, I had created another little intrigue, by having my dear friend from Drew, Binky to send mail to Daddy from me in France. Binky was doing the spring semester in Aix-en-

Provence, France. She would send me blank postcards, and I would write them and send them back in an envelope for her to mail from France to the States. I didn't want the family worrying from not hearing from me for two months. I told them in the post cards that I was traveling through France, and visiting with my friend Binky.

Binky confessed to me that she had told my secret to her no-good boyfriend, when he started pressuring her to have sex, and she told him she couldn't go through the same thing I had. They broke up shortly after that, but she was sure he told his next girlfriend, Judy and he also told Edna.

By that time we had started to call ourselves The Four Horsemen of the Apocalypse, Pestilence, War, Famine, and Death. Our Biblical and classical European exposure made us irreverent and cynical. Gwen was "War" since she would picket at the drop of a hat. Binky was "Famine" because she was so thin and could never gain weight no matter how much she ate. Andi was "Pestilence" because she would often talk in squeaky, pesky voices for our stuffed animals. I was "Death" firstly by default, but then they said I was the antithesis of death, since they had come to think of me as Birth/Mother Earth. We were all living in Asbury Hall, the oldest women's dorm on the campus, but a favorite choice for seniors. The rooms were larger, the dorm was only two minutes from Brother's College, the main class building, and the dorm Mother never heard anything. It was our habit to leave our room doors unlocked. We were welcome to go into our friends' rooms and use their things, borrow food or whatever with their permission. Nobody ever stole anything. Besides, Gwen and I were still invisible except for our growing number of close friends.

Edna lived in another dorm, but it had always been her habit to come by and snoop. When she saw the pictures on my bulletin board, one of me holding my nephew, Jonathan, and one of Teal, I could see the AHA! look on her face, but I didn't say anything. When the picture of Jonathan appeared on the bulletin board in the hallway, I knew Edna had snatched it and placed it there to "expose" me. I took it back into my room and put it away. The picture that I took of Teal on the visit before I signed the papers disappeared, and I never got it back. Gwen and I agreed that we needed to start locking our door. We had discovered most of the keys in Asbury were close enough to fit all the doors in Asbury, so Binky and Andi could still get into our room, but Edna wouldn't be able to.

Years later, Edna was one of the volunteers for the Alumni telethon, and she called me to ask me to give my annual contribution. By then Ralph and I had married, and Joshua was four years old. Edna asked about my children, and I told her Ralph and I had a four-year-old son.

"Don't you have an older one?"

"No, just the four-year-old."

If you're reading this now, Edna, you can say, "AHA!"

I kept that photograph of Jonathan, as my way of keeping Teal close to me. Jonathan was born six days before Teal. And Lynne's daughter Kim was born in October that same year. I watched them both grow, thinking what Teal might be doing at that age.

The only other person who told my secret was my old boy-friend, Johnnysmith. And I didn't learn about it for thirty-five years. When I returned to the States after my Junior Year in Munich, I went to Emporia for the last few weeks of the sum-mer, to be with Daddy, and my step-mother Sophie. I had planned to get my laundry done, get some rest, get all packed for my senior year at Drew, and resolve to sign the final papers re-leasing Teal for adoption.

Johnnysmith heard I was back, probably from Lynne, and he called me. I had broken up with him during my sophomore year before I got to know Ralph. Johnnysmith and I had a spe-cial relationship. I had given him that nickname without his knowledge my freshman year. Even he had joked about being John Smith, almost an anonymous name. When I talked about him to my girlfriends in the dorm, he was "Johnnysmith" all in one breath, until my friends started calling him that too. When they finally met, it was Binky who let the secret nickname out of the bag. He was flattered and a little embarrassed by it, but that became my constant name for him. He was always good to me, and he was easy to be with. It had been a long-distance relationship for most of two years. We had summers and holidays together, and he had traveled to New Jersey to visit me three times. He knew I had dated Billy during my freshman year, and he knew Billy would never have my heart.

It was probably my friendship with Neil Vogel that made me discontent with Johnnysmith, even though Neil was never a romantic interest in my life. Neil was Jewish, and he came to Drew for the UN Semester that spring. His home college was in Indiana, and he had spent the previous semester in Germany. It was Neil who got me thinking seriously about Junior Year Abroad. Neil had never known any black people, and he was thrown in a dorm room with two roommates, one of whom was black.

Bernard Thompson was the Student for that semester from Morehouse College, there to attend the UN Semester as well. Since my roommate Gwen and I made it our business to find the guy from Morehouse, and introduce ourselves, we met Bernard the day he arrived on campus. His roommate, Neil, had a way of tagging along. Neil and Bernard fit right in with our little group of friends who ate dinner together at the long table at the window in the dining hall. Neil and I often got into some serious discussions, with him encouraging me to go to Germany. Bernard was friendly with everyone, except me. I wasn't interested in him even though he was cute, but it bothered me that he behaved as if I wasn't there. I figured it out after Neil started talking to me about his "friend" who liked a girl who was a different race. It was clear he was talking about himself and me. I played along, talking about how the friend shouldn't put any pressure on the girl, and maybe she just wanted to be friends. I decided that I would talk to Bernard about how to make Neil understand there was nothing there; there would never be anything there. Bernard admitted curtly, "Yeah, he likes you," but he didn't offer any advice or any help. I did my best to make Neil understand that I had a boyfriend back home, and there was no hope for him. He said he wouldn't pressure me, he would be happy just to be my friend.

So that's the way it went. The group would go places together. Sometimes eight to ten of us would walk off campus to the diner, and all pile into a big booth together, me, Gwen, Edna (who liked Bernard), Andi, Dick (who liked Andi), Binky, Joe, Neil, and Bernard.

We hung out in the game room, and played big games of hearts -- sometimes hearts with penalties. The loser would have to pick a penalty from the pieces of paper that we had all scribbled beforehand. We had picnics out in the back of the campus. Most other students were coupled off, but people got used to seeing our rowdy bunch together. And we talked about all kinds of things, social, political, traveling.

Even though we agreed to be just friends, Neil still tried to find a way to entice me into a real date. He told me he had tickets to see Jean Genet's "The Blacks" off-Broadway at the St. Mark's Playhouse in New York. He knew I had never been to a play in New York, and that I had an interest in theater. I couldn't refuse.

The play was outstanding, with one small problem. Neil had gotten us seats in the front row. In such an intimate theater setting, it was immediately obvious especially to the cast, that Neil was the only white person in the audience and was sitting next to his black date. The cast took every opportunity within the context of the play to direct their lines at Neil. He was red-faced throughout the whole performance.

When we walked to the subway after the play, we passed a couple holding hands. She was black; he was white.

Neil looked at me sideways grinning, "They're just like us."

"No Neil," I was annoyed. "Remember, we're still just friends."

Neil attempted another date like that when Richard Burton was performing as Hamlet on Broadway. He had tickets for a week night, the night before I was to have an exam. I said I couldn't go because I had to study; besides the Dean wouldn't give permission to go off campus on a week night. In attempting to call my bluff, Neil met with the Dean and got her permission. She thought it would be a wonderful opportunity for me. I was so angry with him for side-stepping me that I still didn't go.

That spring, Martin Luther King came to Drew to speak after he had won the Nobel Peace Prize. We were all excited to see him, although Gwen had met King many times during the Birmingham bus boycott. After the speech she maneuvered us through the crowd so that she and I could shake his hand. Neil was there in the audience, and he said it changed his life.

When Gwen wound up in the hospital with an ulcer, we all piled on the bus together to go to visit her. And when she got better, we made her take breaks to go sit in the grass with the bunch of us. It was the best time we had at Drew.

That spring Johnnysmith came to Drew for the Spring Weekend. Neil knew he was coming, and decided to be scarce. He even volunteered to let Johnnysmith stay in his dorm room for the weekend. When Johnnysmith came to the campus, he was greeted by all my friends, and he would be sharing the room with Bernard. Bernard took one look at Johnnysmith, and his whole demeanor changed. I have never seen anybody so happy to know that I had a black, dark-skinned boyfriend back home.

After that weekend Bernard was a lot more friendly toward me. Gwen reasoned that Bernard just didn't like the idea of my being with a white guy.

After that weekend Neil started interrogating me about my relationship with Johnnysmith. "Tell me about John." I didn't tell him much, and I didn't tell him that there wasn't much to tell. I resented the way he asked. I stopped talking to him about anything for a couple of days until things returned to normal, but it never was normal again. I told Gwen that in some ways I wished that Johnnysmith was more like Neil, or that Neil was black. Neil and I were close friends on so many levels, but I couldn't consider him as a romantic interest. He wasn't attractive or physically appealing to me. He was thin, pale, with stringy blond hair. And as I told Gwen, he didn't have any lips. Johnnysmith never did anything "wrong" but I knew something was missing, that he would always be Petersburg, and that my heart and mind needed to explore more about life. When I broke up with him it was as if I had hit him from out of nowhere. "Neil has something to do with this, doesn't he?" I told him no, because it wasn't the way he meant. Neil would never replace him, but it was Neil who had made me aware that I wanted more.

So that summer after Germany, I was surprised when Johnnysmith called me, and said he wanted to see me. He drove the forty miles from Petersburg to Emporia, and we went out to the drive-in. He said he needed to talk, because of the way things had ended with us. There was a new girl in his life, Audrey. Audrey knew that Johnnysmith had not gotten over me, and they couldn't talk about marriage until he had gotten over me. She was the one who told him to see me. We talked, and we tried making out in the car, but it wasn't working. We both knew it was over. That was when I told him about Teal. He said, "She should have been my baby." I knew Johnnysmith would never have let me give his child away, and that he would have done everything to keep us together. I also knew there was no way for us to return to what once was, and that he would always be "the one who got away."

I saw him once more, in New York City in the subway. It was such a strange twist of fate. It was two days before I was to marry Ralph, and I was on my usual route going home from Newark to Brooklyn. I spotted Johnnysmith from behind, and recognized him by his walk. He had a distinct way of bounding up on his toes with every step. I called him and he spun around, surprised and happy to see me. We talked for a few minutes, my wedding, his job interview, and we hugged goodbye forever. I never saw him again, but I heard he had married Audrey, had four children, and still lived in Petersburg.

As for the secret, I didn't know he told Lynne. I had told

him he couldn't tell anyone; nobody in the family knew except Michael. He must have felt he had to report back to Lynne about our failed date. He and Lynne were close, she knew him before I did, and they were high school classmates. So he told her, and swore her to secrecy. I never imagined that she knew. Even when she wrote me a strange letter after I married Ralph, something about marrying too young, and having a family too young, I thought she was talking about herself, and I didn't know how to respond to that letter.

It started to come out after my son Joshua wrote his screenplay, loosely based on my search for Teal. I had told Joshua about Teal before he went off to college. In his play, Joshua's character meets and falls in love with a girl that he later finds out to be his sister. Joshua tried every angle he knew to get financing to produce his movie, even presenting his story to the family at one of our family gatherings that happened to be at Lynne's house. I sat across the room watching Joshua tell his screenplay story, while Lynne sat on the other side of the room. When he got to the part about the child given up for adoption, I saw the look of recognition on Lynne's face. Her eyes got wide, and her mouth dropped open into a smile. I knew that she knew but I didn't know how. I thought maybe she remembered that summer we spent in the dorm, and surmised that Jimmy and I had had a child. I didn't know, and I didn't ask.

It finally all came together after I found Teal, and I told everybody by email. It was then that Lynne told me she knew all along, and that John had told her. She asked about that letter she had written me. She knew that she had been a little oblique, but she didn't want to reveal directly that she knew. So much for intrigue; it can bite.

Return to New York

Returning to Drew was meant to be a fresh start for me. At least I told myself that. Could I face Ralph? Could I sign those papers? Was there any chance with Jimmy? Could I find a father for my Teal?

I had returned to New York on the Queen Elizabeth (the first one) after spending two weeks in Greece. I intended for the trip to Greece to wrap up the year, and give me a time to reflect and rest. The sun would be good; I could get a nice even chocolate brown, so all the darkened areas from the pregnancy, the lines on my neck, and the line up from my navel would all blend in. I could bake and purify my body, destroying all the evidence.

I had not counted on meeting anyone. I would just as soon have been the hermit, the recluse in the midst of the swinging singles. The trip package was offered by several travel groups that appealed to the young and adventurous. Mine even had an English name -- Club Adventure. The group assembled at one of the secondary train stations in Munich. I was not the only one traveling alone, but of course I stood out, as the only black. Horst came anxiously to meet me. He was traveling with a couple, and the three of them would meet another couple at the next train stop, and a third couple in Athens. Horst was the odd man, eager to complete the set. He had learned some English from black GI's when he had played jazz in a little combo. He brought along his instrument, a Bach flute, what we Americans call a recorder, but clearly an expensive instrument with a richer sound quality. He knew his English was GI-American and not too polished, so it was just as well that we would speak only German.

He and his friends were prepared to have fun. Except for two school teachers in the group, they worked at various odd jobs, just to earn enough to go on the next holiday. Horst had last worked on a construction job in Italy. He was blond and very tan from working outside. It amused him to sit leg by leg with me in my shorts and see that we were the same color. I promised him, however that he had reached the peak of his tan, while I had not even begun mine.

I was thankful to have met him. I was traveling with all of my remaining possessions, having sent the bulk of my things in my trunk months earlier to Cherbourg to be loaded on the Queen Elizabeth. I had two large suitcases which I had to transfer from the train to a bus in Brindisi, Italy, and then to the ship which would carry us as far as Crete, by way of Athens, then to a smaller boat to go to Santorini, our island paradise. By the time he had carried the suitcase the second time, we were speaking on familiar terms.

When we reached Athens, I became the interpreter, helping the group to find the right bus to the Parthenon. The Parthenon was the global meeting place for young travelers from all over the world. There we met the remaining friends of the group. Siegfried and Ursule had flown to Athens because they didn't have the time off to travel by train and boat as the others had.

The last leg of the journey was a seventeen hour boat trip from Crete to Santorini. The trip package had provided for Deck Class -- no bed, but I had paid extra to get third class -- a shared cabin with no provision for food. The others had brought sleeping bags, and planned a jolly time staying up all night. The result was that four of us including me, became sick from a combination of eating bad fish and the swaying and surging of the tiny boat. My cabin was hot and stuffy, with the only relief being given by a tiny fan above my bunk. I spent the first day on Santorini recovering from that last night.

Santorini was worth the ordeal we had been through. We stayed in baked white bungalows that stood in contrast to the crusty soil and black pebble beaches. The volcano on the island had erupted every ten years for as long as anyone could remember, evicting the residents, most of whom returned every time. The main industry was wine, and now thanks to Mr. Konstantinopoulis -- tourists. It was the perfect getaway. With the stark whiteness of all the buildings set against the black beaches, the unfailingly clear blue sky reflected in the purest turquoise sea, the craggy crest of the volcano set in contrast to the soft green of the vineyards, I felt I had been thrust into the middle of eternity, at the end of the earth. When I looked at that sky, I felt that nothing now separated me from my maker.

It was a slow and easy vacation, with plenty of time for just lolling in the sun. There was one tour event planned for each day. There was a mule tour of the whole island, a trip into town where there were a few stores, a restaurant, and a post office. The highlight of the week was the winery tour.

Mornings, if we missed breakfast as we did most of the time, we would have ouzo and water and a roll to hold us until lunch. Lunch always included zucchini, baked or stuffed or sautéed or steamed. Dinner was fish or something that tasted like chicken. Sometimes when the bones were obviously not chicken, we didn't want to think about what it might be. Nights were beautiful and frightening. There was no electricity on our part of the island, so there was no light to blot out the stars. Every inch of the endless clear sky was starlit. I could not spot even one constellation I recognized; there were too many stars.

After the restful week, the return trip to Munich was uneventful, except for an avalanche in the Italian Alps that caused a rerouting of my train through Switzerland so I arrived in Munich a day late, giving me only a few hours before my departure to England. There was not enough time to go back to the dormitory to say a proper goodbye to Ina. I had put it off, thinking I would have another day in Munich. I tried calling her at the dorm, but she was not there and I left a message.

Neil had finished up his studies in London, but he had written to me that when I came through, I could spend my one night in London in his flat. I had no other hotel reservations, and showed up at his flat occupied by ten male students of assorted ages and nationalities. One young man named Nirmal, who was half Ghanaian, half Pakistani, greeted me kindly, telling me Neil didn't live there anymore. His room was taken by somebody else. I must have looked so pitiful with my two big suitcases, that he agreed to help me find a hotel. We went out to a pay phone where I dumped out all of my six-pence, the only coin that could be used in a pay phone. Nirmal called hotels until the coins ran out, and the answer was the same, "No vacancy." It was summer, the height of tourist season. I parked my bags at the flat, and we walked from hotel to hotel until it became dark. As a last resort, I told Nirmal to take me to a police station, thinking they would allow me to sit there for the night. At least it worked in those old black-and-white movies I used to watch with Toni.

"Oh no, Ma'am, you can't stay here." The police were totally unsympathetic, but they made one call, and found me a room. It was rather expensive; four pounds took most of my remaining money. Since I had my transfer tickets to get from London to Southampton, I didn't have anything else to pay except for tips. The room included breakfast so I was able to stuff myself enough to get me through that last day in England. I would have to carry my own bags.

When I boarded the final train, with those same big bags Horst had carried for me, my shoulders ached, and my feet burned from all the walking I had done the day before. I prayed that I wouldn't have to walk far with the bags to board the ship, but it was all taken care of. All luggage with the Queen Elizabeth labels was placed aboard a minibus before I could get off the train. There was no charge for riding the minibus, but I dreaded the scene that might follow. I remembered the time I boarded a bus from the Port Authority in New York, and the porter cursed me out when I gave him all I had, five dimes, for a tip. I saw that the British were too polite. The porter just stared at me in wonderment when I gave him nothing, as if to say, "The audacity!" But I had made it.

The Queen Elizabeth had nothing of the adornment of the Rotterdam. It had been built during the austerity of the war. She had seen her day, and was about to be retired. The amenities

162

didn't matter to me; I was just happy to be able to sleep, to wash my hair and slide between clean sheets. I would have slept late the next morning, but I dreamed of the seven course breakfast.

*   *   *

Senior year should have been a breeze. All my courses would be in my major, and I would be living in Asbury Hall. Gwen and I were roommates again, and Andi and Binky were down the hall. We could fall out of bed and be in class at Brother's Hall in fifteen minutes. We were on the lookout for Ralph on campus, but we soon learned that he was sharing an apartment with Bill in Montclair.

It was almost a week before I finally ran into him. He shook my hand and introduced himself, as if to say he was going to forget he ever knew me, and if there would be anything between us we would have to start from the beginning again. At least that was the start. And I felt my heart go back to the time when he was the older man from the Seminary, and a trusted friend. We talked for a long time, and he listened mostly. I dumped all my pain on him, and cried. His response to my tears was detachment. Maybe he thought I was crying to get attention, but he reacted as if I had a serious problem with depression. And he said I needed to get help. I was stunned by his attitude, dried my face, and went back to my dorm.

There was plenty to keep me busy that year. When I

learned that the second foreign language was no longer a requirement for my degree, and I could have avoided that summer at Howard, if I had only asked, I didn't dwell on it because there was no way to undo it. My advisor, Dr. Schabacker, had given me the position of German Academic Assistant. It was an honor and part of my financial aid package, as there was a stipend to go along with it. I would monitor language labs, grade papers for the first year classes, and proctor exams. Dr. Schabacker wanted me to go for cum laude by doing an independent study thesis. We agreed that my focus would be on comparative literature, and I would have to report to him periodically over the course of the semester. I chose the legend of Dr. Faustus, the man who made a pact with the devil, as my theme, and would include the works of Thomas Mann, Goethe, as well as references to English and American works based on the Faustus legend such as "The Devil and Daniel Webster."

I still had not signed those papers. Gwen kept asking me what I was going to do. I even talked to Ralph about it, and he thought I should get some sense of closure with Jimmy. The last I had talked to Jimmy was when I was at Dana House, before Teal was born. They had notified him of the birth, and I had heard nothing from him afterward. I finally called the number I had for him at his mother's house, and left a message for him to call me. He did call the dorm, when I wasn't there, leaving another number to call. When I called, a woman answered, and I identified myself and asked for Jimmy. When he said that was Paula who answered the phone, and that they were married, I didn't hear anything else. I don't know what we talked about, but I rushed to get off the phone. That was closure, alright. The door was slammed shut. I don't know how I could have expected anything else from him, but now it was certain I had to move on. The name "Baby Mama" didn't exist back then, but I knew I could not subject myself to being a hanger-on. And I could not allow my Teal to live as "that other woman's baby." I called Miss Lipska in New York the next day.

Was it depression or was it mourning? The loss was profound, and I could not get through the days without crying some every day. I wasn't hiding it anymore. I was surrounded by friends who cared about me, and gave me those sorrowful looks of wanting to do something to help me be better. But there was nothing to do but get through it. Ralph decided that I needed professional help with my depression, and offered to pay for counseling. One of his seminary professors had a counseling practice, and I could see him for a reduced rate. While on the one hand, I resented Ralph for still treating me like I was unstable, on the other hand, I thought talking to somebody might help.

I don't know if the sessions helped or not. I was still not able to open up about the whole pregnancy and the adoption. I talked mostly about Ralph and how he had seduced me in his dorm when I was a sophomore. I was probably trying to get even, and the professor got all wide-eyed at the things I said, but he didn't comment other than to say things like, "How did that make you feel?" He took profuse notes. After a few sessions, I just didn't show up anymore. It wasn't helping me, and it was doing nothing for my relationship with Ralph.

There wasn't anyone on campus worth dating at that time. We still had the occasional Friday-night party in the stereo room, where we would dance and talk. Finally Ralph called to make a date. He asked me to take the train to Montclair, and he would pick me up at the station. I agreed, and he picked me up as promised. The date turned out to be a "Booty Call." (That term didn't exist back then either.) I was hurt that he would treat me that way, but he took me home without any argument. When he called again the next weekend, I refused. I told my friends what had happened and there was born the code-name for him for most of my Senior Year..."D.B." for Dirty Bastard.

It was Andi who decided we should go to Planned Parenthood in Morristown. The women from the Morristown affiliate had come to talk to the senior girls in the dorm (we had a new Dean of Women finally) about health care. Apparently the deal was that they couldn't bring pills, but they could talk about health care and pass out pamphlets. Afterwards, Andi got serious with all of us. After seeing the heartbreak I had been through, she wasn't going to have that happen to her.

So, the four of us agreed to make appointments. We all got our first birth control pills. It became a project that gave us a sense of empowerment, and a lot of secret joy. We talked about how we would ever remember to take the pill every day. I was the only morning person, and while I would get up and going for my eight o'clock classes (I still preferred getting them done in the morning), I would be in a partial daze until lunch time. So we agreed we would all take our pills at dinner time, since we would all be in the dorm and could remind each other. Andi referred to it as "Going off to see the Wizard." And we'd ask each other "Have you seen the Wizard yet?" I would say, "It's time for my Wizard trip." Or in especially silly moments we would skip down the hall to the kitchen singing, "We're off the see the wizard."

The only one of us with a steady relationship was Andi. She and Dick had started dating in sophomore year, and they had survived her being away a semester in London. We were simply being prepared; it wouldn't be about any particular man, and we wouldn't be caught unprotected.

We kept to our studies pretty seriously. Gwen was participating in the UN Semester, and was off campus two days-a-week. Binky was working on her senior thesis as well, and had already assembled enough index card references to fill a shoe-box. Our social life was just what we could put together on campus. I would see Ralph sometimes in the Student Union talking with some woman, and I would say under my breath, "Old DB." Sometimes his roommate Bill would come on campus as well. Bill had graduated the previous spring from seminary, and pastored a church in Montclair. He would come over and talk for a while, even when Ralph didn't.

We also managed to squeeze in some activism that year. The voices of freedom came from many disparate tongues in those days, Martin, Malcolm, and Huey. We were just coming to understand the impact of the teachings of Malcolm X after his death. The young turks with their militant stand would have us abandon the non-violence of Martin. The movement was no longer a cohesive unit that marched and sang and joined hands in a circle. We had to listen to all those voices even when they disagreed. Black students all over the country had started demanding more black studies, more black professors, and activities that acknowledged black culture.

By then there were about fifteen black students in the college -- hardly a meaningful presence. Still we organized and decided that we should talk to the faculty members we had a rapport with. I didn't have any problem approaching Dr. Schabacker, "Schaby" as we called him. I told him the background of what we were feeling, what it was like being a black student at Drew, all about Gwen's ulcer during freshman year. Then I asked him what concessions he could make.

I truthfully expected my grumbling was going to fall flat, he would say something to get rid of me and that would be that. Then came the shocker. He had a proposal for me. He had been saving this to talk to me anyway. He talked about how we had lost a German professor to Parkinson's, the new professor was such a thorn in the side of all five of us who had done the Junior year abroad, and he needed to get another professor. He said if I got my Doctorate, he would guarantee me a job at Drew!!! Talk about being careful what you ask for!!

"B-B-B-But!!! I don't have any money for graduate school."

"I can get you a PhD for free!!"

"B-B-B..."

I couldn't talk any further. Schaby was hot on the case, suggesting schools where he had contacts, where I should apply. SUNY at Buffalo and NYU. The train was coming around the bend, and I was on it!!! I had not even thought about graduate school. What now? I got caught up in the whirlwind of applications, and before I knew it, I had been called for an interview in Buffalo.

The head of the German Department at Buffalo was

Schaby's classmate from graduate school, at NYU no less. Between them, somebody paid for my train fare to Buffalo, and I stayed with a married couple who were graduate students. There was ten inches of snow on the ground when I arrived with no boots and they picked me up at the station. They were friendly and gave me the quick tour through Buffalo, and around campus. I didn't ask any "Negro" questions, because I assumed that the population balance would be pretty much the same as at Drew, only a bigger university.

I turned it over and over in my mind. I had no plans for my life after Drew. In the back of my mind, I was thinking about a career in computers. One of my jobs sophomore year had been operating a computer for a project in the economics department, and I had had a vague dream of computers ever since Art Linkletter's "People Are Funny" TV show, when they had a big Univac computer perform some matchmaking. Now I was thinking graduate school, and what would all that mean as a black woman teaching German in a school like Drew?

The interview with the Department head didn't knock anybody's socks off, his or mine. He pretty much that he brought me there because his friend insisted, and I said I was there for the same reason. Getting accepted into their three-year PhD program was not a problem, but he could not get me much in financial aid other than loans. Since it was a State school they couldn't offer much support to out-of-state students. When I met again with Schaby, he shrugged and said we would have better luck with New York University.

The train to graduate school kept rumbling along. I took the Graduate Record Exam, and applied for everything. My interview at NYU was more of a pre-orientation. It was a done-deal before I knew it. The three-year program would require me to spend another year abroad. It was just a matter of waiting for the official acceptance and getting the particulars of the scholarship and stipend. I was excited, but then I wasn't. I didn't know what else I would do if I didn't go to graduate school.

By graduation, Ralph and I were talking more, seeing each other sometimes, but he was still seeing other people. And I saw a couple of other guys I met when we went to New York for parties. Ralph was still "Old DB" in my book. When his family came for his graduation from the seminary, he introduced me to his parents and brother, and we all went out to dinner. He continued to play the game of *"Is you is, or is you ain't my baby?"*

Gwen and her sister Juanita had decided to work in the city for the summer. Graduate school would start for me in September, so the three of us agreed to get an apartment together for the summer. Looking back, it's amazing that it was so easy to get started in New York City. We had a few hundred dollars between us, no leads on apartments or jobs. We checked into the

MOTHERLESS CHILD

YWCA and got the newspapers and we were off on our adventure for the summer. Andi's boyfriend, Dick, had worked in the city the summer before, and he had already lined up a job, and was living in the YMCA. We kept in touch with him for ideas.

All the entry level jobs led us to employment agencies that said the employer would pay their fee. Within the first week, the three of us had interviews, even after telling the agency that it would only be for the summer. In Gwen's case, she had no plans for graduate school yet, and didn't know how long she would want to stay in NYC. My agent told me not to tell the employer it was only for the summer, since I would be there long enough for the employer to pay the fee anyway. They sent me for an interview with a Wall Street law firm as a proofreader.

I had no idea what a proofreader was or what the job might be like, but I went. My major in German Literature was the key. The firm had two proofreaders who were English majors, and they gave me a test for spelling and grammar. They explained the kinds of documents and letters that I would be proofing, and what the workplace was like. The senior partners had their private secretaries, and there was a typing pool of twenty women who handled all the other work. In the days of typewriters, it was a noisy place with all the machines going at once. The proofreaders had a glass-enclosed office in the corner of the typing pool to cut out the noise, but not afford us any privacy. They

172

liked me and hired me to start the following Monday.

Gwen and Juanita had similar success and when we all met back at the Y, we planned our next task -- getting an apartment. This we knew would require finding a sub-lease. Even that proved not to be difficult at all. We looked at a half-dozen places, and decided to take a furnished apartment on 102nd Street near St. Nicholas Avenue. It wasn't a sub-lease, but the landlady would rent it on a month-to-month basis. It was a dump in the middle of Spanish Harlem, but we were young and adventurous. It was big enough that we each had a bedroom and there was a fourth room that we would use for the dining room.

At that time, Gwen was dating my brother Michael, and he came over to inspect the place. Dick, who was still living at the Y thought it was a good place, and thought he could hang out with us there. Unbeknownst to us girls, between Michael and Dick, they hatched a plan for Dick to share the place with us. The dining room had a little bed that would be perfect. And Dick would be our protection in the city. Now imagine Dick and the three of us girls. Dick was a white guy from Worchester Massachusetts, 5'5", and rather pale. I was the shortest of us girls at 5'6", with Gwen at 5'9" and Juanita at 5'10". Dick had been our friend since our sophomore year, and we had put him through the test as the white boy. Now it had to be was humili- ating for him to walk through the streets of Harlem with three

Amazons, who were obviously with him, but who were pretending he wasn't really with them. He played it off by pretending to be our pimp. This arrangement didn't last very long, but even after Dick found another apartment, we were always his girls, and he was our roomie. And when his new roommate didn't work out, he knew he could come and crash with us.

Ralph came to visit once or twice, and he continued to insist that I see other people. So I saw other people. Between us girls, if any one of us met someone, he would have to have friends. Gwen and Michael fizzled out. I think it was a case of each having some kind of fantasy...Michael dating his sister's girlfriend, Gwen dating her best friend's brother. There was no big blow-up, it just faded out. When we didn't have anything better to do, we would go to a neighborhood restaurant and bar around the corner on Amsterdam Ave., have something to eat, and hopefully meet someone to talk to. The first time we went there for dinner, a seven-foot man came into the place, and greeted everybody. They all knew who he was, and I looked at Gwen and Juanita to see if there was any recognition in their faces. They were as clueless as I was. Since we were the new kids on the block, he came to our table and introduced himself. He took our hands in turn and said he was Walter Dukes. We told him our names, and continued to eat. He could tell we didn't know who he was. When he told us he used to play for the New York Knicks, Gwen said, "Oh, **THAT** Walter Dukes," and looked at me snickering. I knew she still didn't know who he was.

So it became a challenge for him. Since we were not admiring fans of the great basketball player, he sat down and ate dinner with us. He seemed to be a nice guy. We told him what we were doing for the summer and I happened to mention the firm I worked for, since I was proud to finally be able to roll off the names without stumbling, "Chadbourne, Park, Whiteside & Wolf." The next day he called me at work and asked me to meet him for lunch. I was floored since I hadn't given him my phone number, and embarrassed to be getting a personal call at that very conservative office. We met and had a quick sandwich, since I had to get back to the office. I surmised that he was checking to see if I was legitimate. When I talked to Ralph, I asked him if he had ever heard of Walter Dukes.

"Oh yeah, he used to play for Seton Hall, and I think he did a couple of years with the Globetrotters." That surprised me!! Then Ralph encouraged me to see Dukes again. "I'm sure he's worth more than I am." I said, "Ohh-kay." And the next time Walter called I went out with him. We had a few dates. He took me to Smalls Paradise, at that time owned by Wilt Chamberlain, and to a couple of popular eating places in Harlem. It was fun while it lasted, watching him and his "public." Once we acknowledged that he wasn't going to get any closer to me, we said our goodbyes.

The next time I went out with the girls back to our neighborhood place, we met Nick in much the same way we had met Walter. He came by our table, we talked, and I gave him my phone number. When he called and asked me out, I agreed, but I didn't feel 100% comfortable with the idea. I went anyway, making sure I had money for a taxi if I needed to get myself home.

What followed, I still can't bring myself to talk about again. I told Gwen and Juanita when I got home early the next morning that I had been raped. They had worried about what had happened when I didn't come home at a reasonable hour, but they didn't know what to do. Now, when Gwen saw me, she insisted that I go to the police. All I wanted to do was scrub myself clean, and wrap myself up in my bed and cry. I didn't know anything about physical evidence; I just wanted to hide. Gwen called Michael, and he came and insisted that I go to the police.

Rape victims get better treatment these days, but in 1967, it was one humiliation after another. I had to go with the police to the apartment, the scene of the crime, to arrest Nick. A woman, apparently Nick's mother answered the door while keeping the chain on. She said she had been there the night before and insisted that the police needed a warrant before she would open the door. (She had been through this before, so it seemed.) That night I had heard someone else in the apartment, but not knowing if it might be another man, or someone else who might harm me, I had kept quiet, not screaming until we left and I encountered some people in the elevator, who looked at me like I was crazy.

The trial was a repetition of the rape. The defense attorney implied that I must have asked for it.

"What color underwear were you wearing."

"Why didn't you scream?"

"He forced his hand down my mouth so I couldn't scream."

"His whole hand?" (smirking)

"Yes!" And I demonstrated, holding all five fingers together and pushing my whole hand into my mouth.

The people in the courtroom watched in sympathy. The judge believed me, and then he made the error of mentioning Nick's prior arrest for another date rape. Then the defense attorney jumped all over the judge for a retrial. Weeks later I had to go through the same ordeal again. This time the DA made the error of giving me the transcript of the first trial while I sat waiting in the courtroom. Ralph came with me this time. When it came time for me to testify, the defense's case was built around the fact that I had my memory refreshed by reading the transcript. And he said the only reason I had cried rape was that I needed to explain my behavior to my fiancé!!! Now he was way off.

"I don't have a fiancé!"

"Are you telling me that the Reverend who came with you today is not your fiancé?"

"That's correct."

All of this harassment of me wasn't necessary in the first place since it all came down to "No Corroboration." No witnesses, no physical evidence, I was still alive and unbruised, my word against his. Case dismissed.

I didn't return to work after the rape. I didn't call in sick; I just didn't show up. It was the end of the summer, and the firm had already paid my agency fee. I didn't answer the phone, and Gwen and Juanita would tell people I wasn't there. It was another loose end of my life that I still regret. But at that time, I couldn't face anyone else.

Michael insisted I needed to move. I would be starting graduate school, Juanita would be going back to Drew, and Gwen had a permanent job. I needed to have my own place. Michael had taken an apartment in Brooklyn Heights, and he thought Brooklyn would be a safer place for me to live as well. There was an apartment available around the corner from Michael, 100 Clark Street. It was a fifth floor walkup, rent-controlled efficiency. At $85 per month, I could afford it by myself with my stipend. I had saved a little money over the summer, so I could buy a studio couch, a card table and chairs, and I was set. I moved in with my clothing and my trunk, and made a palette on the floor to sleep until my studio couch was delivered.

I was surprised when Ralph came to visit me in Brooklyn. He said he wanted to make sure I had a safe place to stay. I felt safe, and at peace there, and from my one window, I had a view of the Statue of Liberty. Then he surprised me by giving me his fraternity pin! This was so inconsistent with the way he had been treating me for the months before, that I sat down on my folding chair and cried. He said the only way he could be sure I wouldn't be getting into anymore trouble would be to marry me.

That was the only time in our years together that Ralph opened up his heart to me. I thought at last I had a safe place to heal.

1968

It was a big year, a year for all time.

I had barely survived a semester at NYU. I knew immediately it was a mistake. The curriculum I knew would be a challenge. There was no more German Grammar course as I had known it. I would have to learn the history of the language working backwards to Middle High German history, and Middle High German language, and the following year it would be Old High German Language and History. Then there was a focus on authors. I chose Thomas Mann for my first, since I had waded through Joseph and His Brothers while at Drew. I would have to read and analyze five more novels by Thomas Mann during the semester. I remembered that reading a novel in German had been so much easier when I lived in Germany and spoke German all day.

All my courses were at night, since the classes were arranged around schedules for working students. The conditions of my scholarship and stipend stated that as a full-time student, I would not take any other work. Although I had lived in New York through the summer, I found that navigating the subways and streets during the dark fall and winter nights was a new challenge. I was terrified. When I finished my last class at ten PM, I would walk with a purpose not daring to look from side to side to the subway, sit tightly in a seat, and run from my stop at the St. George Hotel to my fifth floor walkup on Clark Street. I hated it every day.

And then there was the Nazi factor. I just did not belong; I wasn't German. I don't know why I thought I would fit in. Why did I think I would want to be a German Professor in the first place? These people had roots in Germany, and made me feel every difference. My only winning point was that I could speak fluently. The professors seemed surprised when I asked or answered questions in German. I was as invisible as I had been at Drew. None of my classmates said a word to me. When we had reading assignments from limited journals that were held in the library, I would go in the daytime to do the reading. If all the copies were checked out, and there was one that had not been brought back at the hour the book was due back, sometimes the person at the desk could point out who had one. I would go looking for that person to see if they had just not noticed the time.

"Excuse me. Do you have the reading for the Mittel Hoch Deutsch class?"

When they gave me a blank stare, I would point to it on the table in front of them. Nobody ever handed it over to me. I was an empty space that they would just walk past to return the reading to the desk.

By January, Ralph and I had set our wedding date for June 9, 1968. He was proud of the idea of my becoming **Frau Doktor** Sarah, but when we talked about what would happen the next year, when I would have to return to Germany, he was less enthusiastic about it. I also had to consider what we were going through as black people in 1968, with our new-found pride in blackness. Teaching German would be so incongruous with our style and beliefs. He left it to me to decide if I would continue. He seemed disappointed when I said I was quitting. I told him it was too much like being at Drew. And I didn't even have a professor pulling for me. When I told my faculty advisor that I would be quitting, he asked what I planned to do.

"I want to get a job in computer programming." I had thought it out. When I had searched for a job the previous summer, there seemed to be dozens of openings for programmer trainees. Since the time that I had worked for the Economics Department at Drew, I still had the interest in computers.

"You don't have any experience!"

"There are trainee job openings."

"There isn't any future in that!"

I was surprised he even cared enough to say that. He told me who I needed to see in Administration to withdraw from the

University. It was a fairly simple exit.

I had enough money to live on for a few months. I was always frugal, so the $200 stipend had been more than my monthly expenses. Looking back at that time, it amazes me how easy it was to make that kind of change in my path, and get going without having to call Daddy for help. I answered ads for Programmer Trainee and went on many interviews. There were three companies that called me back for testing and further interviews, and I was made three offers. One offer for a Forms Designer with a bank, I turned down. Then there were two offers for Programmer Trainee, one with the Bell System in Piscataway, NJ, and the other with The Prudential Insurance Company in Newark. I was in the right place at the right time in history. Computer Programming was a new skill and a new discipline that was not even an offering at most Universities. Companies were hiring from Liberal Arts candidates. One Human Resource person even told me they especially like music majors.

The job with the Bell System sounded like a more exciting opportunity, but the commute would be complex from Manhattan, and even after I moved to New Jersey, I would need a car. I didn't even have a driver's license at that point in my life. The Prudential would be a much easier commute from New York, and once Ralph and I were married, I could ride the bus from

East Orange to Newark in half an hour. I started my new job in March, and for the next three months I did the backwards commute. I was always going in the opposite direction of the hoards that arrived in New York in the morning, and went home to New Jersey at night.

I was in the middle of my weeks of training in Pru-COBOL, when Martin Luther King was assassinated in Memphis. I was visiting Michael in his apartment around the corner from me in Brooklyn Heights when we heard the news. I didn't feel the hurt that I had felt with the assassination of John Kennedy. This time it was a jolt of anger. I cried in my anger that this could happen to such a peace-loving man.

The cities quickly prepared for violence with increased presence of police. Newark expected a return of the rage from the previous summer. The next day I didn't go to work. Newark had been calm during the night, so I didn't fear that there would be trouble. I was angry, and couldn't bear facing white people with that anger. I didn't call in. Since I was in training anyway, I didn't know who to call, and at the time, I didn't care about being a no-show. When I returned on Monday, white people were nervous, and nobody mentioned my absence.

Newark was still trying to rebuild after the insurrection of 1967, and the death of Dr. King brought out more patronizing sympathy from the liberals in the suburbs to help fund programs to help the neighborhoods in the Central District. Ralph had his first pastorate in the heart of the Central District, and had already gotten assistance from the suburban churches to remodel the church basement for a teen center.

The job at "The Pru" was good for me. The Pru-COBOL training was only a start, and there was much more to learn on the job. The work group I was in was friendly, and there were many other new college graduates that I came to know well. In those days the office setting was a sea of desks that went from one end of the building to the other. I shared a bookcase and phone with the person in the desk beside me. There was no privacy. The managers had glass offices along the walls. The Pru occupied three blocks in downtown Newark, three buildings connected by tunnels that also connected to the PATH train.

I soon learned that I was one of a very few black professionals employed at the Pru, and when I met people at Ralph's church or at meetings and banquets we attended, they seemed impressed that I had a job at the Pru. I learned also that the Pru was a major bone of contention for the black citizens of Newark during that time of rebuilding. Since the Pru had received major tax incentives to keep their business in Newark, it seemed like a broken promise that few black residents of Newark could even get a job there.

The second big event of the year was my brother Ronald's

accident. He and Vivian lived in California at the time, and had come east to visit family. They were on their way back to California, taking turns driving and sleeping in the car to shorten the trip across the country. Vivian was driving that night passing through Kentucky, with four-year-old Susan in the front seat, Ronald and Ron Jr. in the back asleep and not wearing seat belts. The car hit a patch of ice during a freak April cold spell, went airborne, throwing Ronald and Ron Jr. out of the car. They landed in a stream, Ronald hitting his head, with Ron Jr. nearby. Ron Jr. held his unconscious father's head out of the water until help came.

Ronald suffered a spinal chord injury in that accident, leaving him paralyzed from the trunk down. He spent months in a Veteran's Hospital after being transferred back to California. He was thirty-five years old, and his life expectancy was five years at the time, but he survived almost thirty-six more years, living a very productive life. Ronald earned a PhD in Biomedical Engineering from the University of Virginia, served as a Scientific University Expert at the US Army Foreign Science and Technology Center, and served as Commissioner of Rehabilitative Services for the State of Virginia. We knew it was his faith, and also the devoted care given him by his second wife Anne, that kept him going all those years. We were forever changed by Ronald's life from then on.

1968

*   *   *

Lyndon Johnson was the President of the US that year, and on the day of my first bridal shower, given by the Methodist Minister's Wives, Johnson announced that he would not seek re-election. I remember it vividly, because the ministers were also in attendance at the shower, but they were spending more time in an adjacent sun-room watching television. While I was opening presents, the regular programming was interrupted, and the President made his announcement. Ralph became the loudest and most vocal one to begin talking about the impact of that announcement, and suddenly my bridal shower took a back seat to the political scene. Ralph had a way of taking over the room, and nobody thought to shove the men back in the sun-room so we could continue the party. Even at the end of the party when I was thanking our hosts for the surprise and their generosity, Ralph interrupted to remind everybody that this was an important day politically. Of course it was important. Johnson had been besieged on all sides by the Viet Nam war. There were heightened anti-war protests daily, and even his own party had candidates campaigning against him on a platform to stop the war. But did it have to be in my bridal shower?

When the next major event of 1968 occurred two days before our wedding, I feared I would have to take a back seat again. Robert Kennedy was assassinated on June 6. This time I didn't even cry, I was so angry…what have we come to as a nation, that anybody who fights for justice has to get shot down? It was Bobby Kennedy who as Attorney General during the Civil Rights Era, brought in the National Guard to protect the protesters in Alabama, and the first students to integrate the public schools. He was a visible presence in the fight for Voting Rights. It seemed that our last ally was gone. The train that carried Kennedy's body made stops along the way so mourners could at least see his train. Ralph was there when it stopped in Newark, coincidentally at the same time he was there to pick up his parents who arrived for our wedding.

We seemed the perfect couple. I attended all the church and civic functions with Ralph, and we drew attention, both of us tall with our big afros. Ralph had come to know the playwright Leroi Jones, who was then known as Imamu Amiri Baraka. He led an organization called The Committee for a Unified Newark (CFUN) which behaved like a religious cult with Imamu as their spiritual leader. I attended a few of their meetings with Ralph, and he took the name of Mrafiki, friend. Ralph took it as part of his mission to know all the various groups who had some political influence in the city. Imamu was the founder of the Congress of African Peoples, and we attended the first convening there in Newark. We had such great hope for the growth of the political process for black people. Many cities elected their first black mayors, and Ken Gibson was elected the first black mayor of Newark in 1970. We were also caught up in the symbolism and ritual of the time. At that first meeting, of the CAP, more than one speaker commented that we spent so much time greeting with the latest version of the "Power hand-shake" that the revolution would be over before we finish saying hello. We had our African attire, and displayed pride in our kinky hair.

Ralph became deeply involved in the campaign to elect Kenneth Gibson mayor, and spent much of his time in meetings with other ministers who were active in "the struggle." Even within the Methodist Church there was a growing need ex-pressed by the black clergy to reclaim our roots, through the organization "Black Methodists for Church Renewal," and Ralph became one of the principles in the national organization. By the end of our first year of marriage, I was spending more and more time alone at home nights and weekends.

*   *   *

Daddy retired from his ministry that year, and moved to Georgia with his wife Sophronia (Sophie). Daddy had married Sophie after he recovered from his massive heart attack. She was the sister of his best friend from college at Morris Brown, John Dasher. Mother had been John's girlfriend that Daddy stole from him. Sophie was John's little sister who was still in high school when Daddy was in college. When Daddy's sister died in Forsythe, GA, Daddy went to settle her affairs. I didn't think it was strange at the time that it took several trips to Georgia.

I had been the last to find out they were getting married, and I heard it from my godmother. I was home from Washington for the summer of 1961, and LaVerne, who did her best to help me develop social skills, decided I should visit my godmothers. My brothers would often refer to LaVerne as the matriarch of the family, and she would correct them, loudly reminding us all, "I am not your mother." I don't know how my parents chose the particular people that they did for godparents, but they were all older than my parents. I remember seeing my godfather only once or twice when I was very young. I named two of my dolls after him and his wife. Mr. & Mrs. Fauntleroy were a couple of stuffed gingerbread characters, all brown and soft. One of my brothers must have said that the dolls looked like them, and so the name stuck. They were my next favorite dolls after Sally, but they didn't hold up as well to my dragging them around.

My godmothers were Lizzie Griffin and Carrie Sharpe. Ms Carrie was the Girl Scout leader for as long as I could remember, and she let me join the Senior Scouts earlier than the usual age for Seniors. Ms. Lizzie had directed the children's choir at St.

Stephen's Church. It was on that visit with Ms Lizzie that she let the cat out of the bag. "How do you feel about your Father getting married?" I looked at LaVerne and Lynne, and they obviously knew what she was talking about, while I felt the air being sucked out of me. I must have managed to say something like, "I-I-I didn't know."

When we got back to the car, LaVerne said, "I thought you knew." When we got back home, Daddy said, "I thought you knew." And to both of them I said, "Did you tell me?" *How does a child know when she's loved?* Sometimes I felt that with me it was a case of "out of sight, out of mind." It was easy for them to forget I was still a member of the family.

Daddy and Sophie were married the summer of 1962 in Georgia, after Daddy had done some redecorating of the house on West Street. The house had not seen so much paint since the days of Bishop Payne Divinity School. Mr. Frank Taylor, my friend Yvonne's Daddy, was contracted to do the work, and the spackling, painting and wallpapering. When Sophie came, the house looked better than all the years Mother had lived there. Then at the end of the summer, Sophie went back to Georgia where she worked as the principal of an elementary school. I didn't quite understand that arrangement, but it made sense for me to continue to live with Ronald and Vivian in Washington DC, and continue high school there.

When the church Daddy served in Emporia, VA decided to build a new rectory, Daddy moved there, and by that time Sophie had retired on disability after taking a fall at school. All that time Sophie kept the house she owned in Georgia, so when Daddy retired in 1968, they had a place to go. St. James in Emporia had a big party to honor him on his retirement, and sent them off with gifts. All of Daddy's children except Ronald were there.

When I talked to Daddy by phone after he had moved, I sensed that the life had gone out of him. Maybe it was his heart, or maybe it was the loss of all things familiar to him. He had not planned for retirement and he didn't know what to do with himself. He seemed happy that I was with Ralph, and his baby girl was taken care of. After that last time I talked to him, I said to Ralph, "My Daddy is dying." When we got the call two days later, I knew it before I answered the phone. It was September, 1968.

Joshua's song

When Ralph and I had been married almost a year, he had been pastor for almost two years in Newark. He had started to feel that his mission in Newark was greater than what he could do as a pastor. Newark was recovering from the insurrection of 1967, and there was great interest in the New Jersey Conference in a more global urban ministry. Ralph made a proposal to the bishop to create a position for himself as Director of Urban Ministry as part of the Metropolitan United Methodist Ministries.

Since our church didn't have a parsonage, we had been living in an apartment in East Orange, and were given a housing allowance. When the lease came up for renewal and Ralph was taking his new position, we decided to move to a larger place. I had started talking about having a baby, and we would need more space. This became my first lesson in the importance of "listening noises." I talked about having a baby, and I told Ralph I wanted to stop taking birth control. He was present and listening, and I was taking his silence as consent. It was a continuous conversation on my part, and I thought he was in agreement.

When I became pregnant and told Ralph, I expected him to be happy. When he wasn't, I was crushed. "What have we been talking about all the last four months? Wasn't this why we got a two bedroom apartment?"

"You just married me to have a baby!" That was the first of many statements uttered over the years, that I could never imagine he thought.

Then the disconnect happened and lasted for years. Yes, I wanted a baby. I thought it would repair the hole in my heart. I thought it would get me forgiveness from Ralph. If we argued about anything, his comeback would be, "I don't even know if that is my child." I didn't understand where that was coming from either. He had no reason to distrust me. I never went anywhere but work without him, and I didn't even drive. When I told Michael that Ralph wasn't happy about my pregnancy, he didn't understand it either, but he knew how I had waited for a baby I could keep. Ralph refused to understand. He still had not forgiven me for having Teal.

He referred to Joshua as <u>my</u> child, and when I begged him to participate in his care, there was always an excuse." When he starts walking" "when he gets off the bottle" "when he's toilet trained" "when he can talk better." He was constantly moving the target, and we could never win. Even after I returned to work and there were times when I had to work weekends, he managed to avoid "babysitting," by taking Joshua to visit Bill and Andrea, who were happy to take care of Joshua for a few hours. Emergencies were always mine. The lost days at work were mine. The finding better child care was my job, and picking Joshua up after work was my job, too, even without a car. If the weather was good, I would walk, carrying him. If we happened to be leaving the daycare at the same time as a friend, we would get a ride. If the weather was bad, I would get a taxi.

I gave Ralph my full support for all the changes through his life. When he decided his ministry would be enhanced by knowledge of the law, I said do it. I helped him get what he needed to take the LSAT, and even boned him up on techniques for taking those kinds of test. He had not been required to take the SAT when he entered Morehouse, and he wasn't familiar with taking that type of test. When Ralph applied to Rutgers Law School, he was able to get financial aid to pay his tuition, but for the most part, I was our sole support for those three years. He had summer jobs working with the community program at New Hope Baptist Church in Newark that helped him maintain his lifestyle.

When you talk about lifestyle with Ralph, it was all about the clothes. He always wore suits, and when vests were in style, it was a vested suit. He had more changes of clothes than I did, and regularly made trips to the garment district of New York

City to get the best deals on suits, coming home with several new ones.

We started to talk during this time about returning to North Carolina and the AME Church. Ralph's Dad had been a Presiding Elder in the AME church since before Ralph was born. Ralph had grown up in the AME church, preached his trial sermon in the AME Church, and had been ordained a Deacon in the AME Church. During the time at Drew, he attended the AME Church, but when he sought ministerial work during his senior year, he was only able to find paid positions in the Methodist Church. In addition, he had started to find the system of Bishops in the AME Church, oppressive. I attended an annual conference with him in New Jersey on the day that those licensed to preach were to report to the Bishop. Most of those there to report were either students or were employed otherwise, and had to suck up, lick boots, and otherwise kiss ass for not being available to attend the whole conference. "Yes Sir, Bishop." All the sucking up made me cringe, and Ralph found it demeaning to have to go through that system. By the time we finished Drew, Ralph had transferred his membership to the Methodist Church and was ordained an Elder in the Methodist Church before taking his first pastorate in Newark.

So to return to the AME church would require sucking up again, but at least in North Carolina, the Bishops had respect for

Ralph's Dad, his years in the church, and his participation in getting Bishops elected over the years.

The timing of the move to North Carolina was difficult. Ralph finished his last law school exam early in May, just days before the next bar review class at UNC Chapel Hill was to begin. Joshua and I remained in New Jersey where I worked as a Business Systems Analyst for New Jersey Bell, and Ralph went to North Carolina to establish residency and prepare for the bar exam. By the end of the summer he had taken the bar, we managed to find a buyer for our house in Hillside, New Jersey, and we moved to Fayetteville, NC, where his family all lived. His brother Claud gave us storage space in his garage, and we moved in with his parents. Ralph met with the bishop, officially transferred his membership back to the AME Church, and awaited an appointment at the annual conference in November.

Financially, it would have made more sense for me to remain in New Jersey and continue working until November, but I went along with Ralph's decision to keep us all together in North Carolina. I tried applying for unemployment, but since I had voluntarily quit my job, I didn't qualify. I tried looking for jobs in Fayetteville, but there were no companies who had their mainframe computers in Fayetteville at that time. The big employer in the area was Fort Bragg, and there were no civilian computer jobs at the time. This was before the invention of the personal computer. Some small companies were using mini-computers, but I couldn't get my foot in the door with those. Fayetteville was still in the heart of Klan Country, if you believed the billboard on I-95 as you entered the city limits. It displayed a hooded figure on a horse, and the caption "You are now entering Klan Country."

Joshua started public Kindergarten in Fayetteville, and Ralph and I kept busy just bumping around the house, visiting his childhood friends, waiting for the time we could move to the city where he would have his ministerial appointment. The Bishop had talked about the possibility of going to St. Timothy in Raleigh, and Ralph had also communicated with another graduate of Rutgers, a Fayetteville native, who had already established himself in Raleigh and had a law practice there. We visited Raleigh and agreed it would be a good place to settle.

The Bishop had made no promises. As a matter of fact, it was the custom of the Bishop to surprise ministers with any changes in appointment at annual conference. It was an archaic system that allowed the Bishop to show he had the power over the lives of the ministers as well as the members of the churches who sat through the last day of Annual Conference well into the night when the appointments were announced. There were often gasps and cries of despair, or sometimes applause when an appointment was announced. When the appointment for St.

Timothy was announced as Ralph, a gasp went up from a corner of the audience, an obvious surprise to the members there. The former minister was a childhood friend of Ralph's from Fayetteville, who had been the pastor there for eight years.

We knew it would not be an easy transition. With the conference in November in those days, a holdover from an agricultural society when the crops would be in, and the minister would have the funds to pay his conference assessments, it was a difficult time for families with children to uproot their children in school. "Not easy" blossomed into "downright hard" and moved into brutal. There was a faction at St. Timothy that didn't want a new pastor, whoever he was, and with the help of their former pastor's wife, was determined to make life difficult for him. Fortunately there was another faction who gave us support, and was consistently and genuinely kind to us in every respect. But there were days when it seemed we were in a war zone.

*   *   *

All those years, Joshua was just being a kid with his own unique sense of himself. When he didn't do well in school, we had him tested. Since he always read well, the conclusion was that he wasn't living up to his potential. I felt it was some kind of short-circuit in the way he expressed himself and in the way he often inverted the things we said to him. They had no psychological name for that, and the psychologist's recommendation was that we needed to work with him more on his school work. Years later Joshua was diagnosed as dyslexic. Ralph found it too much to deal with. Joshua just wasn't a mini-Ralph. He wasn't going to be a preacher, and he wasn't going to be the Type-A personality that two over-achievers would expect to produce.

I decided it was my job to expose him to as many different experiences as possible so he could have some choices with his life. It was the 1970's after all, and I believed in the Age of Aquarius. When I was a child the only significant jobs I knew about were teachers, preachers, and doctors. I had ventured outside of that limitation by becoming a computer programmer. I knew there were greater possibilities for my children. Every summer became a new set of decisions for Joshua's time. Ralph insisted on sports, even though neither of us had any aptitude in sports. I played field hockey in school, but I wasn't any good at it. It didn't matter at the time, because our whole team was bad anyway. Ralph had thought he missed his chance at sports because his mother wouldn't let him play football.

So we tried little league, and Joshua had no interest. He dawdled and drew in the dirt when he was on the bench, failing to pay attention to the game. They actually threw him off the team at age seven. We sent him to camp the year I was pregnant with Mark, and Joshua took it as abandonment. He used the time to explore his freedom to be dirty, and hang out in the woods. Even from his early childhood, before he could talk, Joshua would sing, and pretend to talk into a mike that he fashioned from a plastic pumpkin head on a stick. He knew all the songs of childhood, and could recite the words of his favorite stories, including "Marvin K. Mooney, will you please go now!" I suggested Theater Camp, which was a new offering at the Raleigh Memorial Auditorium. Ralph didn't like the idea. The same summer, Jim Valvano had a basketball camp at NC State. Ralph agreed to a compromise -- two weeks of Theater Camp and two weeks of basketball camp.

The theater camp was designed around preparing for a production of "The Sound of Music." They went through auditions, casting, and a production two nights on the stage of the Memorial Auditorium. Once I learned it was the Sound of Music, I had second thoughts, but Joshua was enjoying it in spite of the fact that all of the main players who were cast were blond. I felt humiliated and put down for him, but he was happy to have a part as a singer in the Folk Festival from which the von Trapp family escaped over the Alps. He also played several extra roles including the part of a brown-shirt. Ralph didn't have any interest in attending the final production. Joshua did well, not once missing his cues.

Basketball camp turned out well. It was physically demanding, but since he was in the youngest group they concentrated mainly on learning the rules of the game. The highlight of the camp for Joshua was being in a Mountain Dew commercial as one of "Jimmy V's kids." It was a thrill for him to see himself on TV, even though their only pay was several coupons for free Mountain Dew.

When Joshua later got involved in the drama group at school, Ralph said it was all my fault for pushing him in that direction, but it was clear to me Joshua had found his passion. Ralph didn't attend any of Joshua's high school performances, whether it was the plays and musicals, and especially not his Air Guitar performances. When Joshua went off to college at NC A&T State University in Greensboro, Ralph finally went to see him in a production of "Dream Girls," but he made light of Joshua's participation because he played extras and had one singing part as the "Pat Boone" character singing "Cadillac Car." "Sent my son to a black college to play a white boy."

It wasn't until Joshua did summer theater in Indiana in an outdoor theater production company of "Young Abe Lincoln" that Ralph finally saw the light. Joshua was understudy for the lead black male role, but otherwise played an extra as a young slave. They promised him he would have at least one time to play the lead role. When he finally got word when it would be, we had only two days' notice to travel to Indiana. With last minute air-fares, we decided that only one of us could go, and I didn't feel confident enough to fly and then drive to the back-woods of Indiana alone. So Ralph went, and Joshua made a be-liever out of him. The audience loved him, and Ralph could see the spark and the passion.

The State of North Carolina cut some of the funding for A&T that year and they cut back on the theater department. Their name was "Technical University" after all. Joshua learned during the summer that the head of the small theater department had quit, and gone to work at Virginia Tech. Joshua wanted to follow him to Virginia Tech, but Ralph took charge of the situa-tion, the first time being involved in Joshua's future, and insisted that he transfer to NC Central University in Durham. Central had a long reputation for its theater department and Ralph knew some people who would help Joshua with the transfer and help him get situated in Durham.

*   *   *

It was Joshua's senior year in high school that I told him about Teal. It had been a bad year all around.

It was also my final year in graduate school where I was working on my MBA. Ralph's mother had had a mini-stroke while she was alone living in Fayetteville. His Dad had died a couple of years before. When she didn't answer the phone, and her neighbor had not seen her, Ralph sent someone to get into the house. They found her on the floor in her night clothes, barely conscious. They rushed her to the hospital and found her dehydrated; having an episode of hypoglycemia, and talking out of her head. Her doctor of many years gave her psychotropic drugs to calm her. Within a day she was stable but still talking incoherently about things she saw in the room. Ralph took it upon himself to remove her from the hospital and bring her to Raleigh to his own doctor. The doctor hospitalized her for observation, and changed her medication. Within a few days she was back to herself, and Ralph decided she should come to live with us.

I balked. I didn't need the added responsibility. I wanted to complete my course work for the MBA, and I wasn't going to stop working to stay at home with his mother. Ralph was already absent from home most of the time, and when he was there he was brooding about having a child he couldn't brag about, who was just barely going to graduate from high school. Running the household had become entirely my domain. I managed all our finances, all the cooking, cleaning, shopping, the boys' activities, and went to class two nights a week. Ralph agreed to getting an aide to come in daily, but left it to me to handle the calling, the interviewing, the reference checking, the comparison shopping, and finding someone who could start immediately.

Joshua's Song

Joshua wasn't prepared for college, but he was going to graduate from high school. I decided he had no choice in the matter, and he would go. He could meet the requirements to go to a state school, and I made sure he applied to NC Central, and A&T State. Ralph told him he would study architecture since Joshua had some drafting experience. Joshua said he was interested in theater. This was a continuous back and forth between them.

Finally one Sunday after church, we went out to dinner as we usually did, and Ralph started in on Joshua again about going to college.

"Well, you're not going to spend MY money to study theater."

Ralph had no money put away for the boys to go to college. The only fund was my employee stock options from working for Computer Task Group. I had had it.

"You don't have any money for him to study anything!!!" I stood up from the table and poured my glass of tea into Ralph's plate and left. I had driven separately that day, and went home. I packed a few clothes in a rush and checked into a hotel. I called the house a few hours later to let the boys know where I was. I could hear Mark screaming in the background, when Joshua answered the phone. Ralph would not let me talk to Mark. He said the only way I would ever even see Mark would be to come home. I was defeated. I had not planned this, but it had been in the back of my mind for years that I needed to leave. Now I knew I wouldn't ever be able to leave until Joshua and Mark were grown. And now I had his mother too, to take care of. I went home in silence.

After we had calmed Mark down, it was Joshua who now lit into Ralph.

"You never supported anything that I wanted to do. And you never do anything for Mom either."

Now it was like an Ace in the hole that Ralph had been saving all those years, he told me I should tell Joshua about Teal. While I knew I had been co-opted, I was relieved to finally be able to unload some of my pain from all those years. I showed Joshua the baby pictures, and cried. The intended inference was that Ralph had been there for me, and had taken care of me in spite of my terrible sin. I was still defeated, but I stayed, and the argument about college was over. Joshua went to A&T because his friends were going there, and he took the theater courses anyway.

*   *   *

In 1997 when Ralph died, Joshua had graduated from NC Central with a major in Theater Education after his transfer, but was still missing that passion in his work life. He had had a variety of jobs, and shared an apartment on the other side of town with a friend.

All my siblings came for the funeral, but it was Michael who took Joshua aside and told him now was the time to move to New York. If he was ever to pursue a career in acting, New York was the place to be, and now was the time to do it. It didn't take much time for him to decide, and within weeks he was on his way. When he said good-bye he said to me, "I'm going to find my sister." He said that after losing Dad, we needed to pull together as a family, and that had to include his sister.

Michael had many lifelong friends in New York. Many were students he had taught in public school. He hooked Joshua up with Thomas, whom he had taught in junior high school some thirty years earlier. Thomas agreed to show Joshua the ropes, how to travel the subways, how to find an apartment, where to look for auditions, and how to get a job. Then he allowed Joshua to stay in his apartment for two weeks while he was away on business. Joshua called on his own contacts, friends from college who had been in theater with him. One friend, who was getting more acting work, and could give up his part time day job, recommended Joshua for the job. It was just the thing, half-day receptionist for an investment boutique. It paid enough to cover Joshua's basic living expenses, and gave him the free time to pursue acting.

The bonus of that job was that when Joshua wasn't setting

up conference rooms, or greeting clients, he was sitting by the phone. This was when he started his detective work to find his sister. Joshua called me daily, sometimes several times per day to get the facts, facts that I had nearly forgotten until he started to ask. What hospital was she born in? What was the name of the Home where I had stayed? Addresses, street names, I surely didn't remember. With his persistence and some stretching of the truth he found someone at New York Hospital who would talk to him. He was not able to uncover any specific information relating to me, but he did get a lead on another path he could follow. This went on for months until he finally reached the agency who had handled the adoption. I had not remembered the name, but when Joshua called and asked if it I had heard of "Sheltering Arms," it came back to me. I didn't remember where I had heard the name; the agency wasn't mentioned to me by my social worker, since she wouldn't tell me if there might be prospective adoptive parents. It wasn't until years later when I searched for Sheltering Arms on the internet that I remembered that the ladies who came to play games with us, and taught us to play Bridge at Dana House, had come from Sheltering Arms as a charitable organization. When Joshua said it, I cried from someplace deep and long-forgotten, knowing that he had reached another step in the search. And then it was a dead end. They had to follow the procedures from 1966, the time of the adoption, when no information could be given out until both sides of the adoption agreed to it. Joshua told them I was dying, and wanted to see my child before I died. All they could do was to give me the forms to fill out, giving my permission to be found.

During that period Joshua was able to get some acting work, and to make a lot of friends and contacts in the business. His search for his sister became the plot for his first screenplay. He always imagined the worst thing would be to fall in love with someone who turned out to be his sister, and that became "Loving Kicha." That play, like so many brilliant ideas that are launched in New York City, was reviewed by many people in the business -- producers, writers, actors, who gave their time and input into a project that lasted for many years, but never found the funding to get to the screen. Teal, the daughter I couldn't raise, became Kicha, the sister Joshua never had.

Mark's Song

Mark was the planned child. I made sure to get confirmation out loud and over and over. We agreed that Joshua shouldn't be an only child, and that we had waited so long we feared being too old to see another child grow up. Joshua was eight years old by the time Mark was born, and Ralph was almost forty.

Mark was born with his eyes open, looking around not crying but surveying the room. When they handed him to me, he looked at me in recognition, as if to say, "Oh, there you are," before proceeding to nurse. He was a chunky baby with stubby fingers, fat little toes, and rosy cheeks. Joshua dubbed him "The Incredible Mark" after the latest TV superhero. Since I was able to nurse him for several months until he sprouted teeth, he was much healthier than Joshua, never getting the ear infections, and having no signs of colic. He was a happy baby who woke up smiling and talking to himself.

Mark talked early, repeating everything he heard. In church when I was still carrying him around in a baby bucket seat he would listen attentively to Ralph's loud voice, and repeat "Praise the Lord" when he heard his Dad's loud voice. Ralph had his

Mark's Song

"Mini-me," curly-haired and ruddy-faced.

When Ralph's brother died of a stroke the next year, Ralph slumped back into a depression of non-participation in our lives again. Again there was a moving target of requirements for him to be there for us again. "After my foot heels." Ralph had broken his foot only days before Claud had the stroke. Then it was "after things settle down at church." We were in the midst of a struggle over the land adjacent to the church, a struggle that continued over eight years when we finally sold the old church so we could build a new facility. It became only one more moving target excuse for Ralph.

Ralph did promise that when I went back to work this time he would help with the day care situation. I would deliver Mark to day care in the morning and he would pick up at the end of the day. This would be necessary since I had taken a job with a consulting firm and would often be working on assignments outside of Raleigh. Ralph kept his promise, but often delegated the responsibility, sending his secretary or a friend to pick Mark up after school. Mark didn't mind at all since he was a sociable child, easily went with the changes, and the opportunity to hang out at Daddy's office.

Mark could talk his Dad into anything he wanted, even when I objected. When we had purchased the latest video game machine each of three consecutive years at ever-growing price tags, I thought it was time for Mark to start earning the next machine or he would never appreciate it. Ralph gave in because he was as fascinated by the new technology as Mark was, but only long enough to get it in the house.

Mark was always one to take charge of his own activities. When he started school at Emma Conn Elementary, only a few blocks from home, our plan was for Joshua to get the bus from his middle school that dismissed thirty minutes earlier than the elementary school, get Mark and walk with him home where they would be alone together until we got home from work. That plan became the source of much confusion if Joshua's bus was late, or Joshua needed to stay after school. If they made it home together, they would often fight as brothers do. Mark always managed to tease Joshua about some trivial matter just enough to set him off. They couldn't stand to be together, but they couldn't stand to be apart either.

It was Mark who discovered an after-school program for himself. Many of his classmates were getting picked up after school and taken to the Salvation Army Community Center which was in the neighborhood. We investigated the program and it turned out to be excellent, providing Mark after school care, day camp in the summer, and T-ball competition in the spring, until Mark aged out of the program and applied to be a junior counselor for one year. After he became too old for that,

Mark's Song

Mark found his own summer activities including Boys' Club, and the City Parks and Recreation programs. It seemed that he was growing up the right way with friends who were active and creative.

Mark loved his brother fiercely, even when he was teasing him, he defended him, always making sure Joshua got his fair share even when it was Mark who wheedled something extra out of his Dad. When it came to Joshua's theater activities, Mark was a loyal fan. When Joshua played the villain, a wife-beating mulatto in the melodrama "Flying West," and the audience booed the villain, even applauding when the wife poisoned him, Mark stood up in the audience and said, "That's my brother you're booing."

When we told Mark about Teal, it came in a round-about fashion. We didn't intend to have family secrets, but when there are things you never talk about, they slip into the ocean of forgetfulness. Such was the fact that Ralph had been married before. It wasn't a secret; it just never came up. That is, until Ralph's sister-in-law, his brother's widow, made a comment about "Your Dad's first wife." It didn't occur to her that Joshua wouldn't know. When Joshua came home for the weekend he accosted us with the secret. He was clearly hurt by it.

So in the interest of clearing the slate, I said we needed to tell Mark who was seventeen by then. As Mark came into the room to hear whatever we needed to tell him, Ralph blind-sided me once again by saying, "And you have to tell him about your daughter too." Mark was more stunned than hurt. Even Joshua who knew about Teal already could feel that his Dad was trying to shift the burden of past secrets totally onto my shoulders. Mark took it all in, and in spite of our request to keep it in the family, he had to tell his best friend who had shared his own family secrets already with Mark. But more than anything, this new bit of knowledge went straight to his heart with the promise and personal obligation never ever to give up a child of his own.

Ralph continued to think of himself as having done something noble. Years later when I commented to him how I admired our friend, Jennifer, for managing to live with her husband's "love child," Ralph responded that he had done the same for me. I had to remind him that Jennifer had that little girl at her house every weekend, and that on holidays and family occasions, the child's mother was there too. "And besides," I said, "You never even met Jimmy, and you never so much as looked at a photograph of Teal. It's not the same thing." He didn't mention it again.

He didn't understand my grief, my loss. Could it have been any worse if she had died?

In my early days online before the internet was open to the public, I used an 800 baud modem to dial-up to work from home and handle database problems during the night and weekends when it was my turn to be on-call. Mark took to the computer the way a fish takes to water, and he along with his friends, found online message boards using my modem. After someone told him about the board at NC State, we found more lists with phone numbers to dial up to other boards. I found a message board for people looking for birth parents. It was 1986; Teal was twenty years old. When I found a board for parents who had children who died, I read posts on that board into the night. After I received the call from work after midnight when the database maintenance jobs ran, it might take fifteen minutes to resolve the database issue, and in my still-waking midnight longing, I would read the posts from mothers who wanted someone else to understand how deep the pain went for a child who had lived only months. How deep was that pain?

Working on the Building

It should have been our dream house. I wasn't looking to build a house, but I liked looking at the house plans in the Raleigh Times every week. That one was intriguing with the wall of windows facing South – a passive solar house. It would be flooded with daylight in winter, with the clerestory windows letting in light from the top. Ralph said, "Let's build it," kind of on the spur of the moment the way he always did with decisions that I would have to spend months mulling over. I never knew what he might have been privately thinking about. I would have gotten books on passive solar design and had a clear idea of the square footage, and the practicality of it. It was so rare for Ralph to do something new, that I knew I had to send for the plans in the mail.

By the time the plans came I had gotten books on passive solar design and had a little understanding of what the various factors would be in building that house. Ralph decided we needed to talk to a solar engineer, and he found a graduate student at NC State who was willing to sit down with us. Ralph hired him as a consultant to advise us on building the house.

This was all so crazy, like I was being swept up on a train

to Buffalo all over again. At the time we lived in a perfectly nice house in Sherwood Forest in Raleigh, three bedrooms, all brick, on a half-acre lot with huge loblolly pine trees. It was perfectly fine for us with Joshua and Mark. The next thing I knew, Ralph was talking to his cousin Rebecca about buying some land. We had just come to know this first cousin of Ralph's mother who happened to live in Raleigh on several acres of land that had been passed down through the family. Rebecca had become a dear friend and confidante, who talked to Ralph many times every week about a variety of topics, politics, family history, her children, and the ins and outs at St. Augustine's College where she was on the faculty. She had come to treat Ralph as another son. All he had to do was say the word, and they arranged a deal for us to buy a lot from her on State Street. It was the closest lot to the dirt road that led up to Rebecca's house in the woods, and was situated such that we could get the Southern exposure we needed for the solar design.

That's the way he was. If he wanted something he could get it. He knew enough people that he could find a connection to anything and anybody. It was during that time he was being harassed by a Nigerian student at Shaw University. He had done some legal work for a number of African students who had gotten into trouble with speeding and traffic tickets, and he had met this particular young man on one occasion. Then out of the blue this man started sending letters demanding that Ralph give him back the 1.8 million dollars Ralph allegedly stole from him. The letters escalated into phone calls at all hours of the day and night, and then the guy took out a personals ad in the newspaper, making the same demand for his 1.8 million dollars. At the beginning Ralph ignored him and wrote him off as some kind of crazy man. Nevertheless the phone calls started to rattle us all. Ralph finally called his seminary roommate, Bill, who by then was a Congressman from Pennsylvania. He merely had to give Bill the details, and within days it was determined that the young man was in the US on an expired student visa, and he was deported to Nigeria. I joked with Ralph for months about "my share" of the 1.8 million dollars.

We kidded about the money, but at the same time I worried about where the money would come from to build this house. Our mortgage was comfortable. I knew that house would probably triple our housing expenses. Ralph always said, "The Lord will provide."

We took our time paying off that lot, and I hoped that Ralph wasn't working on going forward quickly. Before I knew anything, he was having conversations with our friend and neighbor Lawrence, about a builder, the same builder who was constructing the church Lawrence and his family attended. Lawrence had a leading role in that building project. Ralph went and inspected the work being done on that church and saw that the builder, Mr. Jarvis, was an excellent mason, doing beautiful brick and stone work on that church. Lawrence had recently started construction on a new house near our lot, using that same builder.

We took a trip to Greenville to meet the builder, and see some of the houses he had built. The first building he showed us was a parking deck. That should have been the first red flag. It was clear Mr. Jarvis was an expert mason, and could build structures that would withstand the worst weather we could have in central North Carolina. Then he showed us some of the houses he built, with the permission of the owners living there. I asked about the design of the houses, since they were rather haphazard with odd cubicle spaces and dead-end halls with unused space, and because we had already selected our plans. He assured us that he would sit down with us on our plans and could build whatever it was we wanted. I noted that the walls of those houses were all paneled; either wood paneling or various vinyl wall liners -- another red flag. We passed by one house that he told us he built, but he said the owners didn't want to talk to him -- another red flag. The last house he showed us had not sold, and was the only one that was more than one story. The staircase in that house was a pre-fabricated spiral staircase. The kids thought it was great, and they wanted one like that, but that was another red flag. We left a copy of our plans with the builder and he promised to get back to us with estimates.

I didn't want to do this. There were too many red flags. Ralph insisted Jarvis could build our house for less than anybody else could (he didn't have any other estimates), and we just had to look at his fine masonry work to see how competent he was. (*The train to Buffalo was boarding.*)

It's a good thing I don't remember dates, and I dare not dig through all the papers and invoices and receipts connected with the building of that house to find the dates, but it took over a year for Jarvis to build a shell of a house -- all brick with a fantastic stone front, and two beautiful fireplaces. But there were no rooms, no stairway in 2 ½ stories, and we were paying on the construction loan at a mighty interest rate, until it was clear Jarvis would not finish that house.

One day, Cousin Rebecca called me at work to tell me she was worried about Ralph, because she had seen him at the worksite, going through the house. The last she saw him he was sitting on the brick front steps with his head in his hands. I left work early to see what was happening, and he wouldn't talk to me. He just looked forlorn like he couldn't see a way out of this. He finally said something about giving it up. By that time we already had a lot of money sunk into that house, in addition to the construction loan.

"We can't keep paying for two houses. We have to finish

this one and sell our old house," I insisted.

"But Jarvis is gone," was Ralph's forlorn response.

"Well he hasn't done anything in weeks anyway. We can get our own workers."

"What? Be our own contractor?"

"Yeah!" I was resolute. I had seen enough technology projects that had gone awry, late and over-budget. I knew the only way to dig us out of this mess was just to do it.

So it was decided!! All the brick work was done. We needed carpentry, drywall, plumbing, electrical, roofing. My determination not to give up ignited Ralph to do what he did best, find the experts and delegate the work. I didn't know where the money would come from, but he found a way to do that too. He got personal loans for thousands of dollars from every friend he could tap. They all knew he was good for his word. The site was soon buzzing with workers, more than we had ever seen when Jarvis was in charge. As the walls came into place, I took on the decorating tasks, the wood finishing and painting.

Every day after work, I picked Mark up from day care, went home and cooked a quick dinner, and by seven PM I was back at the house in my bib overalls, working. Some days I had friends who came to help. Ralph was home with the kids, doing what he did best on the telephone. Most of those spring and summer nights I had only my radio for company, while I climbed up and down the ladder to sand and stain the exposed beams in the living room and dining room. I worked until my fingertips were brown with walnut stain, and the sun went down. On weekends there were others who came to help paint the bedroom walls. We had to pay someone to paint the high walls above the beams, the stairway, and up to the clerestory windows.

By the end of the summer it all came together, enough for us to pass building inspections and get an occupancy permit. The basement wasn't completed -- we didn't even have steps down to the basement, so that door had to be key-locked to prevent anyone from accidentally falling down into it. The deck wasn't built, so the three sliding glass doors intended to enter the deck had to be barred. The floors that would eventually be covered with slate to catch the solar heat in the southern exposure were bare concrete in the living room and dining room. The garage had no door, just a gaping opening. We couldn't access the garage anyway because the driveway wasn't paved, and we still had piles of construction debris around the yard. We moved in as it was, and put our old house on the market.

We moved in, while we still had carpenters installing cabinets and baseboards, and eventually the stairs to the basement. I still had my evenings in bib-overalls, but with the luxury of air conditioning and electric lights. We made it through by the grace of God, and with some comic relief. Our house was a neighborhood spectacle -- the largest house in sight in a neighborhood of single-story bungalows. Everyone showed an interest in seeing how the house was coming together. There was one white man who had made our house part of his daily constitutional for months. Ralph called him "the little general" because he was short, and walked with a cane that he used like a swagger stick, more for pointing and probing than for support for walking. After we moved in, the little general continued to show up every day, but because the doors were locked, he couldn't make his inside inspection. Finally after being shut out for a whole week, he rang the doorbell. I went to the door and had to position myself in the vestibule to block him from barging in.

"Excuse, me, did you want something?" I was trying to be polite in spite of my annoyance.

"The neighbors feel like the house should be open as long as it's owned by the bank," he insisted with the arrogance of the man in charge.

"This is our house." I smiled while slamming the door in his face.

Then there was a very nice lady who came with her children one Sunday afternoon, and rang the bell. "Would you show us your house?" She was very polite about it, so I had to smile back at her, and say, "Sorry we're just moving in."

"When you get it all decorated, will you invite the neighbors to come and see?"

"Uh, no," I said while giving her my best twinkle-eyed smile, nudging her out of the door.

And the carpenters who were only coming on Saturdays because they had regular jobs during the week, one day decided to bring the whole trailer park family, who came with their folding lawn chairs -- the wives, somebody's Momma, and a nine-year-old boy, who just thought they could have a picnic in our unfurnished living room with the concrete floor. Ralph had to have a word with them, and they appeared insulted that they weren't welcome to watch Jim-Bob work.

It took another year before we could afford to install the slate floors, finish the deck, the garage and lawn, and carpet and panel the basement. I could finally stand back and feel proud of the work we had done. Joshua's friends would come and admire the house, and the teenage-boy conclusion was that the house was the best in the neighborhood, and Joshua could get girlfriends just by living in that house. Ralph stayed stuck in "house is not finished, I can't let you in" mode until the week before he died, when he suddenly decided the house was beautiful.

It was a learning experience that Ralph put to good use. A few years later we were ready to build a new church. All the things we did wrong in building the house, we turned into smart planning for the church. The fund-raising was still paramount, and Ralph was again able to draw from his friends in the ministry, even using thousands from our personal funds to finally reach the day when we could dedicate the new St. Timothy.

In all those years of fund-raising, I often called on the support of family as well, and many responded with donations. When we used the "Tree of Life" to raise funds for the landscaping required by the City of Raleigh, many friends and family members purchased leaves to be inscribed on the tree. It was then that Michael said I reminded him of Mother, "You're living out Georgia Gordon's life." I didn't have the opportunity to know her from an adult perspective, and never received adult advice from her, so whatever it is that drove my church involvement, it must be deeply rooted in the genes.

Ralph's Song

We are soldiers in the army,
We have to fight although we have to cry.
We have to hold up the bloodstained banner,
We have to hold it up until we die.
- Folk Tune of the Civil Rights Movement

I could have learned so much from Mother's death, if they had let me be part of it. I didn't know she was dying. She could have told me. She could have told me how to face God, face the end. She paid off all her bills before she died, but she didn't know how to include me in that payoff.

I didn't know about faith then. Episcopalians don't "get saved." Salvation happened on Calvary. Salvation is free. It was enough to grow up in a community of faith to be included in that. I learned about faith through Ralph. He truly believed God would provide, would always be there, and never forsake us. And he lived his life that way. I would worry about where the money would come from to send the boys to college, when it seemed that every spare cent went into the building fund for St. Timothy AME Church. When I reminded him that he had no pension, he would say he would work until he died. Besides, "The Lord will provide."

He was like a man driving through a mountain range. He could see the big picture, all of the glory of God's abundant grace, but he couldn't see me in the blind spot beside him. I felt that he intentionally kept me in his blind spot, always walking three steps ahead of me. If I complained, he would say I needed to walk faster. If we found ourselves at a social gathering, talking to a few people, he would absentmindedly move in front of me, cutting me out of the circle. Even when we devised a signal that said, "Hey, I'm still here behind you," he would still shut me out, keeping me in that blind spot. He was involved in bigger things, while I was just along for the ride.

* * *

When he was dying, I was sure that it was the steroids that caused his strange behavior. He hardly slept, and would toss and turn through the night and every hour or so would ask me to get the nebulizer to give him a treatment so he could breathe. The days were calmer. He still went into the office for as long as he could, and would call me to come pick him up. He was too weak to drive and have to walk from his parking space to the building. He would say things to me out of the blue that made me sure he had lost hope of recovery. One day it was "I don't want to have hospice." Another time it was "After I'm gone, maybe you can find someone to love you the way you deserve to be loved." I couldn't respond to those statements since I still had hope that he would survive. When he couldn't rest during the day, he called everybody he knew and told them that he had cancer, and that he loved them. When he ran out of people to call, he would call mail order houses and buy things he didn't need, or just talk to the person on the other end.

During one of those buying sprees he decided he needed a new car. His Mitsubishi Diamante was in excellent shape. He bragged about how well it drove, saying that all the miles he was driving back and forth to Orange County were making it into a better machine. Since we hadn't expected to be at that church in Orange Country for long, I had suggested that he keep that car until we weren't driving so much.

Then one afternoon I got a call at work from Ralph's secretary. He had asked her to drive him to the Lexus dealership so he could buy a new car. She knew how sick he was, and she thought I should know what he was doing. I went out there immediately, and tried first to reason with Ralph, and then with the salesman. I took the salesman aside and told him, "This man was too weak even to drive himself out here. He is dying of cancer. You can't sell him a car." The salesman's logic was that he's a grown man, and unless I have some court order to say he is incompetent, what can he do? I called Ralph's friends to try to reason with him, until he finally agreed to come home. I asked him to allow me to take him to get checked out, and if the doctor said he was all right then we could talk about the car.

I had to sign him into the hospital that time because he couldn't even remember his Social Security Number, and he was behaving erratically. The Bishop came to see him during that visit to the hospital. He was in town to meet with the trustees of the AME homeless shelter. When the meeting was over he asked them to take him to see Ralph in the hospital. Bishop Worthington was the most humble of all the Bishops that I knew – a regular guy who didn't require being set upon a pedestal. He came and prayed with Ralph, and when he had finished, Ralph broke out in song, *"We are soldiers in the army."* He remembered his days at Morehouse when he participated in student sit-ins at a lunch counter in Atlanta. That was one of the songs of the movement, and all the ministers who came with the Bishop joined in. It was the last time Ralph was able to sing. When the ministers left, the Bishop hung back and placed a hundred dollar bill in Ralph's hand. I nearly fell off my seat, having become used to Bishops who always had their hands out, and here was one who gave. I thanked him and held his hand as he left.

That was one of the few calm times during that hospital visit. He was determined to get out so he could get that car, even to the point of threatening a nurse. The staff feared that he would become violent, strapped him into a straight-jacket, and called a psychiatrist for consultation. I was there when the psychiatrist came, and told him I thought it was the steroids, that had been prescribed by the first pulmonary specialist. On top of that prescription his chemo cocktail also included steroids. The psychiatrist agreed to cut back the steroids and also prescribed something to calm him.

When he was finally released from the hospital, his friend Craig insisted that I should let him get the Lexus. By that time I was simply worn down, and gave in, knowing he wouldn't be able to drive that car for long, if at all.

Two weeks later we were back to the hospital. It was Easter Sunday, and Ralph had gone to church, but was unable to conduct the service. He had bought that last suit to wear, and he had become too thin for it to hang properly on him. He had worked on his sermon all week, "Can't no Stone Keep my Jesus in the Grave," but when the moment came, Presiding Elder Coble stepped in, knowing Ralph was too weak to deliver. Mark had to help me get him home, up the stairs and undressed. He was unable to rest at all and finally asked me to take him to the hospital.

I wasn't prepared for him to be dying. I had done the research, and best case I read was a five year survival. I was sure he would have two years. By Monday, the head nurse told me that his vital signs were not good, and she didn't expect him to make it through the week. During that time I was talking to my sister Toni every day, and she read it in my voice, the combination of despair and panic. Toni took it upon herself to say, "I'm coming." Toni herself wasn't very mobile. She was suffering from Parkinson's disease, and got around with the help of a wheeled walker, but that didn't stop her from buying an airline ticket to North Carolina. When she told me she could get a good rate to Greensboro, I told her that Greensboro was too far away, and she needed to come to Raleigh. She wouldn't listen, and by the next day she was calling me from Greensboro that she was getting a bus to Raleigh.

I told Joshua and Mark how grave the situation was, and they came. The doctor was prepared to mark Ralph's chart as DNR, Do Not Resuscitate, and I had to explain to Joshua and Mark that we had Living Wills that say we don't want to be kept alive by extraordinary means. Mark asked, "What if they find a cure?" We just held on to each other and I told them both, that a cure for lung cancer may take years and we can't put your Dad through holding on in that condition.

The friends came, the true ones and the hard-time ones. (They always warn you about the good-time friends, but never about the ones who only show up when something bad has happened.) The clients he had helped with employment complaints, the ones he had helped to get jobs, and the church members for whom he had done free legal work, they came. The legal colleagues came, and the ministers came, and the halls of the hospital were so filled with people, you would think we were in the courthouse or in the lobbies of Congress. One friend took me aside and said all this traffic was keeping Ralph from resting. I said, "He will rest soon enough. You know how Ralph is about telling everybody all of his business. This is his time to say goodbye." That was the last day that he could talk. The next day his tongue was swollen, and his throat was blocked with mucus. I had to turn the visitors away except for family. I was sleeping on a lounge chair at night, and going home for a shower and fresh clothes for a few hours in the afternoon when someone else could be there to sit with Ralph. I didn't actually call anybody other than family to notify them, but the word was spread.

That was the time of the Hale-Bopp Comet, which was brightly visible even during the day from the parking lot of Rex Hospital. It gave the visitors something else to talk about when they came to visit. When the reports came of the mass suicide of the Heaven's Gate cult, who thought their souls could take a ride on a spaceship they believed was hiding behind the comet carrying Jesus, that just added to the buzz in the parking lot. When Ralph's friend Bill finally got the word that Ralph was gravely ill, he came as soon as he could and arrived late one night when that comet was all ablaze. Bill didn't say much, and Ralph could hardly talk. After all their years together of brotherly arguments, there were no words.

We planned his funeral, Ralph and I, in those last days. He chose the hymns, and I selected the Scripture that he had repeated over and over on the phone to his friends in those last weeks, Psalm 91. The verse that says, "You shall not be afraid of the terror by night, nor of the arrow that flies by day," still resounds in my head. He asked if I would get Greg to sing "My Soul is Anchored in the Lord," and insisted that his pastor from St. Luke in Fayetteville should preach his eulogy. That was the protocol.

They moved him to Palliative Care on Saturday, where he could have a home-sized bed, and a television with a VCR, where we played videos from family events. Toni hung in there the whole time. I don't know where she slept. She didn't want me to worry about her, so I can only hope that my friends made sure she had whatever she needed. When I talked to Ronald, he suggested that I have Toni there with me when Ralph passed. He said her peaceful spirit would help to usher him in. By that Saturday night they were giving him morphine against his objections, but he was in too much pain otherwise. And the nurses settled us all down, Ralph, me and Toni around nine o'clock. My doctor had given me a prescription to help me sleep. Joshua and my friend Clarestene stayed in the family lounge down the hall.

He passed away on Sunday morning, April 6, 1997. When the time came to select the suit for his burial, I wanted to use the last one he bought. Ralph had searched everywhere for that suit. It had become a game he played with the salesmen in all of his favorite clothing stores, when asked if they had a suit, "double breasted six-on-three." Half of the salesmen didn't know what he was talking about, and Ralph took pride in explaining, "Six buttons each side, but only three are fastened." Nobody had one, but said they would order it for him. He kept looking until he finally found one in his favorite Bachrach mail order catalog. He had become so weak that I had had to dial the number for him, and left him alone to have a long conversation with the customer service. Ralph told me later the Bachrach order had come to $900 for the suit and fifteen ties.

I left it to Joshua and Mark to make the final choice since they insisted that it should be one that he usually wore on Sundays, a dark navy pin-stripe. After quiet deliberation they added one of his favorite white-on-white shirts and a tie with red, just the splash of red Ralph would have appreciated. Even in death, at his last outing, Ralph would be the dashing figure they always knew.

*   *   *

I didn't grasp until he was gone, that I had been missing a

part of me all those years. I loved him through it all, and I know that he loved me the best way he knew how. Ralph supported me in my personal sense of ministry that had nothing to do with being the preacher's wife. He announced to the congregation that "Sarah is going to be herself, not someone to be set apart." I taught Sunday School and sang in the choir, not as the "First Lady" but as just another member who loved children, and loved to sing. And even with that role that I took for myself, I knew I was driven by something outside of myself. It's funny how all my Daddy's children, all of us "bad" preacher's kids, continue to be active in some faith community. When I sought the help of a grief counselor, she determined that my grieving over Ralph's death went back to something earlier. I didn't tell her about my loss of Teal, but I did talk about my loss of Mother, and my feeling that Mother died before she was finished. In all my church work, I wasn't being the "First Lady;" what I was doing was finishing for Mother.

The Burden of Unforgiveness

One thing I admired about Ralph was his ability to forgive others, even though he never forgave me. And sometimes I think that what got us back together after I had Teal, was his need to forgive me, even though he never could, and my need to be forgiven, even though I never was.

Even now, long after his death, when his so-called friends have betrayed, even defiled his memory, I know that he forgives them. But he never forgave me.

Even in his delirium from the steroids when he was dying, he remembered how I had hurt him. He confused the rape with Jimmy. He said he knew he could trust his first wife, Marian. She would come and get him out of the hospital. He couldn't trust me because I had gone off with that guy while we were engaged, and gotten myself raped. As if I wanted to be raped, and we weren't engaged at that time, and we weren't engaged when I met Jimmy either.

"Remember, you told me we should see other people."

And it was rape!! The judge said he believed me because he read that guy's rap sheet, even if it wasn't admissible, those two previous date rape arrests. The lawyer even got another trial because of that judge's statement.

Ralph came to the trial. He saw how they tried to make me look like the guilty one.

"What color underwear were you wearing that night?" As if wearing a red slip meant I was asking for it. And that lawyer told the court the only reason I went to the police was that I had cheated on my fiancé.

"I'm not engaged!!! He's not my fiancé." And they tried to bring Ralph's character into their whole defense.

Two trials, two times facing cross-examination and all those questioning eyes. The observers in the courtroom believed me. There should have been a jury, but the defense asked for a panel of judges. I could see the sympathy in their faces, how they nodded "Yes" he could get his whole hand in my mouth to stop me from screaming. Even the men in the courtroom nodded yes, as I showed how my hand could go into my mouth. And the women were disgusted with the defense attorney's attempt to paint me as a slut who hung out in bars.

The judges found him not guilty. No Corroboration.

The trial was worse than the rape. And Ralph never forgave me.

I hung on all those years forgiving his indiscretions, the "groupies" who would show up at my house when they didn't see my car. All because I needed his forgiveness, because I never forgave me either. Not for betraying Ralph, because it wasn't a betrayal.

I never forgave myself for giving my Teal away.

When I wrote to Jessie, her adoptive Mom, I said I couldn't regret giving her away because Jessie had given her a much better life than I could have. She gave my Teal the life she deserved and dreamed to have. I could never regret that. But I can't forgive the separation, the hole it left in both our hearts. The gaping hole and the hard question, "Why did you give me away?"

2002

It was a year that fulfilled all promises and hopes.

I had not planned to remarry; I had already been blessed with more than I had ever hoped for. I would be content to live the rest of my life alone. After Ralph died, and I finally sold that big house on State Street, I settled into down-sizing. My little bachelorette pad was perfect for one person. It had taken longer than expected to sell the house on State Street. The first year, I took the standard advice of not making any major moves, but I prepared the house for selling. The clean-out was enormous, since we had lived there seventeen years, and the kids had stored up every toy and gadget. Even the ones that broke were stashed away in the attic or one closet or another. Every Thursday was the day when the garbage collectors would haul away big trash items, and I would start on Wednesday afternoon to move boxes of old toys, record players, boom boxes to the curb. The scavengers in the neighborhood soon noticed there might be some good working things in my pile at the curb, so that by Thursday morning my pile had been reduced considerably. Even the trash collectors might spot something if the scavengers missed it, and ask if they could hide it behind a tree to come back and retrieve after they finished their route.

Then there was the remodeling. We didn't have a pretty kitchen in that house since we had done the finishing ourselves, so I set about to remodel it. I knew a new kitchen would add to the value, and at least make it more marketable. Besides, the project would give me something to keep my mind busy.

Another major move that I deferred was any change in my job. By the time Ralph died I had been promoted to a Director position. The previous Director, my boss, had been promoted to Chief, and offered his position to me, telling me that if I didn't accept, one of my peers would be his second choice. I had been happy in my position as Manager of Technical Support and Database Administration, so any further advancement was beyond my dreams for my career. I knew I could handle the Director Job, and that it would make me the highest ranking black person, and the highest ranking woman in the agency at the time. I knew I would be a "credit to my race," as straight-arrow as I always was; I would never get into any of the audit problems that plagued many people in State government positions. I had many friends throughout other State organizations who would give me the support and guidance I needed. Besides, my boss' second choice, while a competent manager, had a reputation among his black employees for showing racial favoritism, and I thought I could protect the Section from any further racism if I took the job. It seemed a no-brainer.

After being Director for two years, we had been through several reorganizations, and I was working sixty-hour weeks in addition to taking work home nights and weekends. I had lost so much time with my family, and I felt guilty. Mark was off to NC A&T State University for his freshman year, and we had put Ralph's mother into a retirement home since she had reached the point that she could not be left home alone.

A close friend at work asked if I planned to continue to work. I had not figured out yet if I could afford to quit. Ralph had substantial life insurance that would certainly protect me from poverty, but maintaining that big house would also factor into the equation. I told my friend I just didn't know. I knew my heart wasn't in it anymore. I had made my mark, and didn't have anything to prove anymore. I knew I needed to give it at least a year before doing anything drastic. My friend suggested that I could retire in place. He had done that already himself. He was close to completing the thirty years of service he needed to retire, and he knew he wouldn't get any more promotions; all he needed to do was to "meet expectations" to keep his job until he was ready to leave.

Eventually the reorganizations were cutting positions, and the head-count in my group was being cut, first through attrition, but we knew that a Reduction in Force was imminent. Some of the responsibilities I had taken on in research and development were moved to a new group, and the management of the State contract for applications development was moved to a new position. I had been doing the work of several people, and they were gradually stripping my responsibilities down to management of a steadily shrinking group anyway. It was easy to cut back to forty-hour weeks.

It was also during this time that the State started to ramp up its internet support. The agency was the Internet Service Provider for State government, my Section was beginning to develop internet applications, and I encouraged my staff to become internet savvy. During Ralph's short illness I had searched for as much as I could find on squamous cell lung cancer, and had read enough of the survival statistics to know what to expect from Ralph's illness. I had hoped for two years of survival, but he made it only ten weeks.

When I reached the point of ramping down my personal work activities, I was using the internet in my spare time at work. In those days there was little of entertainment value, but after Ralph had been dead over a year, I did sign up on a site I thought would help me find old friends from high school. I received an email from someone I knew from school. He was a class behind me, but we had been part of the same circle of friends. He had once been the boyfriend-of-the-week of one of my Ingénue Club sisters. We started to write emails regularly, and after several months we began a long-distance romantic relationship. It lasted over a year, until I had sold the house and quit my job.

That relationship opened the door for my social life. I only wanted someone to date, go to the movies with, have dinner, maybe travel with if it became serious, but I was having no luck at all meeting anyone in Raleigh. I let all my friends know it had been almost three years since Ralph died, and I wanted to date. Most of my male friends had in fact been Ralph's friends, and when I would ask specifically about some man I might want to meet, they would say he wasn't good enough for me. My single girlfriends were being protective of their own short supply of men in our age group.

That left me to my own devices, and I began joining several internet "social networking sites" for black people. That unlocked a new world for me technologically. I found myself more interested in web development than in the people on those sites, and I had great fun developing web pages, and learning every new trick I saw being used online. I had a few "first dates" that didn't develop into anything. By 2001, I was frustrated that I had not found someone I could call and say, "Let's go" somewhere, other than my circle of girlfriends.

After I finally quit working in 1999, on a whim I had

earned my real estate license and was working part-time selling real estate. It gave me some structure to my day, so I wasn't spending the whole day on the computer, and I had some different people to interact with. I was traveling occasionally, going at least once a year to visit Joshua in New York, and seeing a few Broadway shows. My life was pleasant, but still empty. I was active in church, teaching Sunday school, singing in the choir, serving on the Trustee board, but it wasn't enough.

Finally in February 2001, I joined Match.com. When I filled out my profile and got my first list of matches, the top of my match list was a gentleman from Maryland just off the Capital Beltway. I sent him an email, and we started exchanging emails, and then started chatting online several times a day, until we finally met. Edgar was a charming man, retired and widowed, and not at all the physical type I had as my wish list. He wasn't tall and thin, not the distinguished gentleman Ralph was, but he was round and cuddly and we found it uncanny how much we thought alike about so many things, to the point that we were completing each other's sentences. When we chatted online, I would type something at the same time he was typing the same thing. I thought he was the right fit for a date.

I had heard enough horror stories about people meeting online, that I had already made it my practice to check someone out before ever meeting in person. I told Ed it was what I needed to do. It was simple to use free search resources to find a man's tracks on the internet, especially if he had an unusual name. When I first exhausted free searches, if I was serious about meeting someone, I would pay for a search that would give me a report from an assortment of public information. Mostly I wanted to know if the man was who he said he was, he didn't have a criminal record, and he was single. One gentleman I had met the year before on Blackplanet.com, I found had $50,000 in Federal tax liens. He had mentioned that he was working extra overtime to pay off some debts, but I met him anyway. He was pleasant enough, but I knew there would be no future for him. Another man I had chatted with had such an unusual name, that I found numerous online newspaper reports about his divorce struggles and an incident that involved a gun. I removed him from my chat list after that.

The first time Edgar came to visit me in Raleigh, he arrived with flowers and candy, just like in the movies. I found him to be thoughtful, attentive, and fun. Since he was retired, it was easy for him to come to Raleigh, and I went to Maryland to visit with him. One of our early dates was my niece Bertha's baby shower in Washington, DC. Since the party would be near his neighborhood in Maryland, I invited him to come. He came with the intention of taking me out to dinner after the party. He didn't mind at all being with my family, and he was right at home playing with the little kids in the family, even talking baby-talk to the babies. I soon decided I could learn something about being thoughtful from Ed. He was always surprising me with little things. When he found out I liked Marshmallow Peeps, the Easter candy, he would hide some in places where I would be sure to find them. Whenever we went anywhere, he never walked ahead of me, always beside me, holding my hand. When he said I had a "good holding hand," I thought how Mother would have agreed. Edgar even had the right moves, protecting me through crowds and guiding me through doors. I found him to be a great dance partner who can apply just the right pressure to the small of my back while he turns me with the other hand. Not bad for a fluffy old guy. He was such an easy traveling partner, and an old Pro at travel. Part of his job before he retired required him to travel to government sites all over the country. He kept a separate supply of toiletries packed, along with a hot pot, cups and supplies for tea. He had frequent traveler memberships in several airlines, cruise lines, and hotel chains. He had even gone to school to become a travel agent, but stopped short of graduation when his wife died. We had gone on a couple of trips together before we planned a trip to Cape Cod for Sept 11, 2001.

We were driving north on I-95, listening to Tom Joyner in the Morning, changing radio stations all the way so we could continue listening to the syndicated show all morning as we crossed state lines. Then we heard the report of the first plane hitting the first tower of the World Trade Center. They reported it as some terrible accident. When the second plane hit, it was clear we were under attack, and Tom Joyner gave his program over to network reporting. I was driving at the time, and we stopped at the next rest stop. By that time the Pentagon had been hit.

I felt a swirl of feelings, fear, terror, confusion, not knowing where we should go and who we should call first. Joshua worked in Manhattan at the time, and I tried calling him, but no calls were going through. "Circuits are busy." I tried calling my brother George in Washington, and got the same message. Ed and I talked about turning back, but we didn't know if we would find mass confusion in DC. We both lived alone, and our accommodations were paid for in Cape Cod, so we went on. By that time all bridges and tunnels into New York City were shut down, and northbound traffic was starting to back up. We checked the map at the rest stop, and decided to take the Tappan Zee Bridge around the north of Manhattan. When we reached the point north of the city where we could look back, and could see the cloud of smoke where the Twin Towers once stood, I heard a small voice of stunned despair that was my own. Then it became more personal. "They" had attacked "my" city. I was numb for the rest of the ride to Cape Cod. I was able to call Washington, DC later that day, and asked George to try to reach Joshua. He was able to get through the next day.

I was in mourning for the rest of that week in Cape Cod. I watched the news reports on TV as much as Ed would allow me. He tried to get some sense of normalcy back while we walked on the beach or rummaged through gift shops. When we visited the Kennedy museum at Hyannis, and I saw the life-sized pictures of John Kennedy and his young children, it all came back on me, the same feelings I remembered from 1963 the day that John Kennedy was shot. Ed was my rock through the whole thing. This was a major event for him as well, but I knew he didn't feel it in the same personal way that I did. He allowed me to mourn, allowed me to just be, even if it locked me into my own personal silence where he didn't dwell. By the time we were ready to leave Cape Cod, I knew this was the man I wanted to keep in my life.

I could say that the great events of 2002 were ushered in on December 23, 2001 at the birth of my first grandchild, Mark's son Markus. Mark and Jill had dated for about a year before she became pregnant. He was still enrolled at A&T State, but was not making progress toward graduation. With Jill's pregnancy he decided he needed to work full-time since he would have a family to support. We/they talked about marriage, but it wasn't happening. Jill waited a long time before telling her family in New York that she was pregnant. When her due date in December came near, Mark asked if I would be there for the delivery. I said I would, but I knew we might have some conflicting dates in December. The family was having Christmas dinner at Lynne's house in Maryland, and Ed had asked me to spend Christmas with him. His house was only minutes away from Lynne's.

I knew by then that Christmas was extremely important to Ed. The first photos he had sent me before we met were not of him but of his house, all decorated for Christmas. His decorations were the kind that would light up the sky to guide the way to his neighborhood. My idea of Christmas decorations had been a tree, some garland here and there in the house, and some electric candles in the windows. By the time he had decorated his house that year, he had brought me some extra lights he had so I could light up the shrubs in front of my house. I had never had so much Christmas lighting before. He had also told me of how he had broken up with his previous girlfriend after two consecutive Christmases when she had been out of town and had returned to spend more time catching up with her girlfriends than with him. So I knew if I was to continue to see Ed, I would have to celebrate Christmas with him.

Mark called me early on the morning of December 23, to

tell me that Jill was having contractions. I told him they should go to the hospital, and to call me if they kept her. It was a Sunday morning, and I was getting dressed to go to Sunday school. I took my cell phone with me and told my class I might have to leave on short notice because I had a grandbaby coming. When Mark called again, he sounded desperate to have me there, so I left my class and drove on to Greensboro, an hour and a half away.

I had expected to wait at the hospital in the waiting room and get periodic reports of Jill's progress, but they insisted that I should come into the birthing room with them. I had never witnessed a live birth except for my own children, so I was as excited about it as Mark was. Mark was a little apprehensive, fearing he might get dizzy or faint from the sight of it, but he hung in there, even cutting the umbilical chord. Jill watched through the mirrors and delivered a red-faced little boy with fat cheeks like his Daddy's. He even had a head full of thick hair the same way Mark did when he was born. It was a day of elation for all of us. Jill went home the next day, and I was able to visit my grandson again before I drove to Washington early Christmas morning. I told Mark & Jill that I needed to go, because I thought Ed might propose. When he gave me an opal ring for Christmas, that wasn't accompanied by a proposal, I was afraid I had misread the signs. I started to wonder how much time I should give the relationship if he didn't propose. But he surprised me when he did at the stroke of midnight, New Year's Eve.

Ed and I were married April 28, 2002 in the church Ralph and I had built. We had spent weeks of planning and deciding the major question. Where would we live? I was willing to move, as was Ed. At first he suggested that we keep both of our houses, and live in both places. I didn't like that idea, because we would never be "at home" together. His house would always be his house, and mine would be my house. He agreed and we spent most of March looking at houses in the DC/Maryland area. Then when we looked at similar houses in Raleigh, it was clear we could buy the same house for far less in Raleigh. I told Ed that if we spent our entire budget on housing, we wouldn't have money left to travel. That cinched it, and we signed a contract to build a house in Raleigh. By the time we married, Ed had sold his house in Maryland, and moved his furniture into storage, awaiting the completion of our house in Raleigh.

October 24, 2002 started out as an ordinary day. We had moved into our house at the end of August, and by then we had our furniture in place, completed window treatments, and wall-papering. Ed was a handy man, who worked in the yard and in the house. That was another bonus about him that I didn't learn until we were married. He could fix or build just about everything. He had constructed the valances which I covered with fabric for all the windows in our house. He had already laid out plans to double the size of the deck, fence in the back yard, and build a gazebo. He was always very busy. We had an easy, happy life together. Some days I would wake up and pinch myself to make sure I wasn't dreaming. Ed and I thought alike on so many things, that there was never an issue. Our life was more than I had ever hoped it could be. Even my friends commented on how different my life turned out to be with Ed. It was as if I had a whole new life.

I was into a daily routine of going to the office of Jordan & Hicks Realty, leaving home around ten AM and returning shortly after noon. Ed would tease me about my "work hours." It was all I needed to work part-time. I took calls at the office in the morning, and if I had a client I was working with, we made contact through my mobile phone. I turned my phone off at night before I went to bed and turned it on again in the morning after breakfast. When I turned on my phone that day, it buzzed that I had a voice mail. The message was, "I'm trying to locate the mother of Joshua. If you are the mother of Joshua, then you are the mother of my wife." I felt myself go weak, and I sat down. The rest of the message gave me phone numbers to call Glenn. I ran downstairs, my face flushed and my eyes already starting to flood with tears. Ed looked at me wondering what was wrong. I said, "You have to hear this", and I played the voicemail again. Ed was overjoyed. He hugged me, and said, "When are you going to call him?"

I spent the next hour on the phone, talking to the husband of my long-lost daughter, my Teal. He told me how she had gotten my name from the adoption agency, and Joshua's name. Of course it was all that information Joshua had given when he was hot on the case. Since that time he had moved, I had moved and I had changed my name. It was providence that I had given the phone company my mobile number as a forwarding number when we moved from my bachelorette pad, to temporary quarters while we waited the completion of our house. They would give out that number for six months. Another two months and the trail would have gone cold, and Glenn might never have found me.

He talked, about how they had met, and married. They had a baby boy. When he told me she had gone to Duke University in Durham, I thought how close she had been all those years. "And to Duke Medical School." I felt my heart leap. She had had a good life, and reached her full potential. All those years, I had worried she might have spent her life in foster care with no one to love her. We talked on, and I cried, such joy. Ed was listening to my half of the conversation, so when I hung up, he hugged me as tight as he could. He was happy for me. "Who are you going to tell first?"

I had to call Joshua. He was as excited as I was. "Did you tell Uncle Michael? Let me tell him!" I don't know what we did the rest of that day other than talk on the phone. When Joshua reached Michael on his mobile phone, he was in a public place, and Joshua told him to sit down first. When he told him, Michael cried out loud, so the people around him came to see if he needed help. He laughed and told them they were tears of joy.

Over the next few days, I exchanged emails and photos with Karen -- they had named her Karen Teal. We talked on the phone, and there were more emails, covering the details of our lives, more emails, and more questions, some I could not answer. But I knew this for sure. Finding my child after almost forty years was the greatest gift I could ever imagine.

The hard part I thought would be telling the rest of the family. Michael was the only one who had known the secret all those years, or so I thought. I decided to try to do it online using instant messenger. I sent everybody an email, and set a date and time for everybody to be online for my announcement. George and Michael were used to online chatting but nobody else was very adaptable to the idea. My brother, Bobby called me and tried to guess what my announcement was. "You're not pregnant are you?" He was always the kidder. Then he went down his list of possibilities: Someone getting married? Somebody sick? Somebody have a new job? Then when he said, "You found a long-lost relative!" I had to laugh and say he was right, but I wouldn't tell him anything more. So he decided to get his grandson, Robbie IV who was in college at the time, to be his delegate for the online chat.

I did get the announcement out, but the expected questions didn't come. LaVerne called me later to express hurt that I had gone through so much by myself and didn't feel like I could tell anybody. She felt that she had failed me as a big sister. I reminded her that I knew she had her own issues that she was going through at the time. Ronald called with a similar response. He felt he hadn't been there for me during the time I lived with him. He should have been the one I went to. Lynne hadn't been online that night, and she called me the next day to tell me she knew all those years after John Smith had told her and sworn her to secrecy. We laughed together about how the secrecy and intrigue had worked in the family. I hadn't told her myself because she had become pregnant soon after I did, and she and Dick had gotten married. I hadn't wanted to lay my own different choice on her. If only I had known that they would have been there for me.

It was only a few weeks later that I saw the film "Antwone Fisher." It was based on a true story of a young man who had survived a horrific childhood growing up in foster care. Joshua and I saw it separately, but when we talked about it we had had the same reaction -- that could have been Karen's story. Joshua, ever the dramatic one wanted us to have a family reunion with Karen just like the one in the movie. We both hoped that after I finally met her in person, that it could be arranged.

Finally, the weekend before Christmas, Edgar and I went to Atlanta to meet Karen and her family. I felt like I was preparing for the biggest date of my life. We had talked on the phone, we had shared pictures, but that physical contact was going to finally put it all together. Ed was all ready with his video camera. We hugged and cried, and I held one more precious grandson. I told Karen that it was as if someone had made a deal with the Devil on my behalf, and I had been given all the riches I had ever wanted. Of course, I knew it was the Lord who let his face to shine upon me had blessed me with more than I ever deserved.

Epilogue

"WASH ME"

Y ou've seen those words scribbled in the dirt on the back of many-a-car. "Wash me." Most likely the car belonged to someone who has regular dealings with young people -- a teacher, coach, principal, minister. And it was the young people who decided that the car was dirty, and they needed to give a voice to that car, as if to speak and say, "Wash me." It's usually done in fun, but just think of the audacity of it, for them to put themselves in the position to judge when something is dirty.

I know you can drive a car, and get used to the way it looks, as it gradually gets a thicker and thicker layer of grime. It goes with the territory. You drive the streets and roads that collect dirt or you may have some dirt sprayed on you from an open dump truck that is carrying loose dirt. And don't let it rain or snow. That mixture of water and grime encrusts itself on the exterior of your car. You have to notice it then, but you might decide to wait until the storm is over, or the snow is melted before you decide to get out the hose, or take your car to the car wash.

Meanwhile those pesky kids are around to write in the dirt, "Wash me."

Can we get so oblivious to our own dirt, that we can't tell for ourselves that we need to be washed? Can we do our regular housekeeping and still be walking around with something unclean? Can we smell our own bad breath or our own funk before people start backing away? Do we know our own sin? Or do we think we can wait until the storm is over in our final hour to seek forgiveness. And yet we know that we all sin and fall short of the grace of God. Once and for all, can I go to Christ and say, "wash me?" How can I regret those decisions however wrong or foolish, if they brought me this far in my life, if my decision to give you away gave you a good life? Still, for my sins, I beg, "wash me, forgive me, love me."

Writing this book helped me to purge the pain of those years. It was never intended to absolve my guilt or to transfer my guilt to anyone else. The writing was painful. I hope the reading has not been painful for those who learned the secrets of my life.

> *What can wash away my sin?*
> *Nothing but the blood of Jesus.*
> *What can make me whole again?*
> *Nothing but the blood of Jesus.*
> *by Robert Lowry 1826-1899*
> *Hymn #405 AMEC Hymnal*

CPSIA information can be obtained at www.ICGtesting.com
Printed in the USA
LVOW07s1542140615

442432LV00001B/246/P

9 780615 212944